RELEASING
~THE~
WARRIOR
WITHIN

D0890773

RELEASING
~THE~
WARRIOR
WITHIN

ROBERT L. BRYAN JR.

MILESTONES
INTERNATIONAL PUBLISHERS

RELEASING THE WARRIOR WITHIN:
The Power of Prayer...The Power of Praise

ISBN 0-924748-50-8
UPC 88571300020-8

Printed in the United States of America
© 2006 by Dr. Robert L. Bryan

Milestones International Publishers
140 Danika Drive NW
Huntsville, AL 35806
(256) 830-0362; Fax: (256) 830-9206
www.milestonesintl.com

Cover design by Steven Plummer, www.idesignhomepage.com
Cover image by istockphoto

1 2 3 4 5 6 7 8 9 / 10 09 08 07 06

ENDORSEMENT

Dr. Robert Bryan has explored the methods, dynamics and principles of spiritual warfare. In doing so, he has created this tool for believers to develop them in spiritual warfare.

Dr. Stanley Williams, Sr. Pastor
Fire Of The Word Christian Faith Center Church

———

The Bible says in 2 Corinthians 10:4 *"For the weapons of our warfare are not carnal, but mighty through God to the pulling down of strong holds."* The only way to insure success is to be equipped with the Word of God by praying the Word and fasting. Know that the warrior in you is going to be equipped to do justice in the Kingdom of God once it's been released. This book is a motivational tool that was released by God to the man of God, to the people of God. **Read it and do it!**

Dr. Angel Smith
Kingdom Destiny Ministries
Detroit, Michigan

———

Dr. Robert L. Bryan Jr., has truly captured the essence of spiritual warfare. This book will revolutionize man's thoughts on spiritual warfare. I highly recommend this book to every believer.

Frederic Pinkney
Pastor and Founder, Joshua Faith Christian Center
Jacksonville, Florida

ENDORSEMENT

Releasing the Warrior Within, written by Dr. Robert L. Bryan, Jr. - what a wonderful book. Profound, moving, insightful, passionate, educational and on time. It is a skillfully written and engaging volume which reflects the heart of God. Dr. Bryan is passionate about his subject yet thoughtful and balanced in his approach towards the matter of spiritual warfare.

The book is based on scripture, written from the heart and inspired by sensitive pastoral love for God's people. Those who read this volume will be enriched.

Bishop Steve O. Campbell, PhD, - Senior Pastor
Word of Life Ministries International
Steve Campbell Ministries
Brick, New Jersey

RELEASING
~THE~
WARRIOR
WITHIN

ROBERT L. BRYAN JR.

MILESTONES
INTERNATIONAL PUBLISHERS

TABLE OF CONTENTS

CHAPTER ONE

GOD IS A GOD OF WAR

The LORD is a man of war; the LORD is His name
(Exodus 15:3).

Most believers know God with respect to all of His compassionate and empathetic attributes. Many Christians understand the real concept of and can readily visualize how God's character can have multiple effects on various people. For example, most people—particularly believers—willingly accept the concept that God is a God of mercy, love, patience, grace, power, holiness, faithfulness, and immutability. These are attributes that most people have come to expect and feel comfortable with about God. For the most part, each one of these characteristics displays a somewhat passive aspect of the nature of God. So we can contentedly live with these notions.

Although these attributes are definitely true concerning our God's character, He is not limited by the passive aspect. God has another side that is equally as redemptive, beneficial, and effective as all of His more commonly accepted attributes. Few believers know God as a God of war. And one of the main reasons, if not the primary reason, that some believers live in a perpetual state of defeat is directly related to their lack of knowledge concerning this powerful quality about God.

Now, I've been around church folks for a very long time. I'm not a novice to the church scene. Equally beneficial to me is the fact that neither am I ignorant of the street scene. So I have a greater than fundamental knowledge of both arenas. In the church world, most believers are cocky and arrogant, believing that they pretty much know everything there is to know about God, His church, and living in victory. I realize that learned people don't make generalizations such as "most church people" or "most worldly folks," as I just did. Those kinds of presumptions under most circumstances get everybody into trouble.

However, in this area I feel a bit safe, since I have taken a mental census of church people's behavioral patterns over many years. Although I'm not a famed statistical researcher like George Barna of the Barna Research Group, I am a watchful eye and have had the privilege of pastoring and prophetically ministering to thousands of people throughout the past 15 years or so. What I have seen is that people who really love God, who really believe that they know what I am going to say, have rehearsed all the one-liners that church folks memorize. And yet they live in defeat.

For the most part, the devil is really excited that he has believers exactly where he wants them—in a position where they no longer seek God or knowledge. The most dangerous position in the world is that of sincerely believing that you know everything you need to know. Not only are parishioners in this position; unfortunately, many pastors and other fivefold ministry gift leaders have actually stopped seeking as well. The point at which you stop seeking is inevitably the time the devil launches his attack against you. And in all probability he will win over and over again because you are trying to defeat a high-tech demon with industrial knowledge. That will never work!

The Bible says in Matthew 6:33-34, *"But seek first the kingdom of God and His righteousness, and all these things shall be added to you. Therefore do not worry about tomorrow, for tomorrow will worry about its own things. Sufficient for the day is its own trouble."* You see, the only way you can live without worry and feel totally confident that everything in your life will be taken care of is by seeking. If you don't seek, then what you neglected to seek will equate to the knowledge that you so desperately needed in order to conquer in your previous as well as your next battle. Victory comes through a continual process of seeking.

According to Matthew 6:33, you are expected to seek God and His kingdom. But you don't seek God merely for the sake of seeking. That's the mistake most Christians make. We do so many churchy things without having an intended goal or objective in mind. When you seek God, you are seeking Him to get a clearer understanding of how His kingdom operates. Once you have mastered that knowledge, you will become invincible.

Do you think there is anybody who actually knows and properly lives out every aspect of the United States Constitution? Allow me to answer that for you: No! All the people who are considered to be experts on the Constitution are not considered to be experts because they are experts. They are considered to be experts because they

Victory comes through a continual process of seeking.

continue to study the Constitution to discover hidden truths and to uncover the mindset of the original forefathers who drafted the Constitution. All the individuals who contributed to the original document are now dead. So a Constitutional expert cannot expect to have an interview with James McHenry, Roger Sherman, Benjamin Franklin, William Patterson, Rufus King, Charles Cotesworth Pinckney, or Gunning Bedford, Jr. All of them have been dead for a couple of centuries now.

So how does one get an idea of what these men originally had in mind when they wrote the Constitution? The only way to discover that is to read the Constitution over and over again and to study other supporting materials relevant to the subject. If you are not willing to do that, then you will never be considered an expert in the field. It is no different with God's Word and His ultimate design for our lives. We must read the Word of God first and foremost. But we also need to read supporting works to help us better understand His Word. Listen to tapes and CDs to feed your spirit so that you will have a defense mechanism already in place when the enemy comes against you.

The fear of the LORD is the beginning of knowledge, but fools despise wisdom and instruction (Proverbs 1:7).

So many ignorant people say, "All I read is the Bible; nothing more." Doesn't that sound really spiritual and holy? Well, as holy as it sounds, it is also foolish. The Bible says in Proverbs 1:7 that the fear of the Lord is the *beginning* of knowledge. Notice that it does not say that fearing the Lord is the ending of knowledge. After you fear the Lord, and after you submit to His will, and after the tithes and offering have been sown, and after the message has been delivered, you are going to need knowledge to help you become a conqueror in every area of your life.

Would you read the Bible to help you understand stocks and investments? Of course not. You would read *The Wall Street Journal* for that information. Preferring *The Wall Street Journal* over the Bible in matters that deal with stocks and bonds is sensible. God tells us to seek Him and fear Him. In the process of seeking Him and fearing Him, He gives us clear directives as to where we should go, whom we should connect with, what resources we should read, and how we ought to conduct ourselves in every given situation. When we listen to His heart on every matter, not just some, we find ourselves to be the victors we were born to be.

When you try to spiritualize everything and neglect knowledge, the Bible calls you a fool. And your rejection will eventually cause a major destruction in some area of your life. That's why this book was written; it is to help halt the onslaught of the enemy in various areas of your life. Enough is enough; it's time to let the devil have it!

One thing that greatly grieves me is when I see my fellow Christian brothers and sisters of all colors, sizes, and shapes and of various persuasions all over the world live so beaten down. I am here to tell you that the knowledge of God, the knowledge of Who He really is, will free you forever.

Yes, He is the Savior, He is the Healer, He is the Deliverer; but He is also a mighty Man of War. Once you receive revelation on this much-misunderstood topic, you will forever be liberated from the shackles and chains that the enemy has put on your mind. You've become far too comfortable living as you are. I have written this book to make you very uncomfortable. You do not have to be comfortable with defeat. You can have success in life all the time once you recognize Who God is—a Man of War.

GOD—PACIFIST OR WARRIOR?

When you and I have to choose between pacifism and war, the obvious choice is pacifism. This is especially true when it relates to the potential of innocent lives being destroyed by scared and angry soldiers. But when we view things through the eyes of politics, we often make improper judgments about God and His holy church. Contrary to popular belief, God is not a Democrat. Before you start cheering me on, let me add this: Neither is He a Republican. You may think, *God must be an Independent or simply bipartisan.* Wrong answer! God does not associate Himself with any political party because He is not a politician. God rules by His own name, by His own authority, however He chooses to do so.

God does not have a board of directors. He doesn't even have a leadership team. He doesn't operate by a poll system. And God does not rely on the electoral vote to keep Him in office. Now, I'm being a bit facetious, but I am trying to convey the message to you that God stands alone. He is all in One. *"Hear, O Israel: The LORD our God, the LORD is one! You shall love the LORD your God with all your heart, with all your soul, and with all your strength"* (Deuteronomy 6:4-5).

So does God promote pacifism or war? That depends on the situation. It solely depends on which realm we are speaking about. If we are speaking about the spiritual realm (the area I am most capable of addressing), then God promotes war. He will do everything in His power to protect His greatest interest—His creation. As violent as it sounds, God will kill your enemies. Now, don't get all bent out of shape. God's not into killing people. But He is very much into stopping people's negative progress against you.

The whole battle that you face in life is not a natural battle, no matter how much you think it is. It is a totally spiritual battle. Health problems, financial problems, marital problems—all appear to be natural quandaries with natural solutions. Think again. Each one of those areas is spiritual at its very core. The devil knows what kind of influence you will have when you conquer those areas and many others. Your salvation is really not about you, as much as you may think it is. I know that you are saved and on your way to heaven. But heaven should never be a believer's objective. In fact, heaven is a pretty simple trip. All you have to do to get there is die.

Your objective should not be heaven, but other people.

Others should be your objective. You are saved to help others learn how to live victoriously by following the example and principles of Jesus and His Word. To that end, the devil will fight you to stop your progress in helping others recognize the truth. What truth is that? You don't have to be financially broke. You don't have to have a horrible marriage. You don't have to live in a perpetual state of sickness and disease. The generational curses that you discovered do not have to be your reality. You don't have to be a drunk, live with grief, feel guilty all the time, or feel that your service to the Lord is never enough.

All those things are strategic areas where the enemy has launched his attack. More than anything, God wants to destroy Satan's work. But He cannot. Why? God can't kill Satan because you are too closely juxtaposed to him. And if He kills Satan, you too might be destroyed in the process. You ask, "Wait a minute, Dr. Bryan. Do you mean to tell me that I am in Satan's quarters? That I am so closely connected to the devil that it's working against me?" Sad to say, you are just too close.

That does not mean you are not faithful to the work of the Lord. It does not suggest that you are not saved, sanctified, and Spirit-filled. It doesn't mean you aren't effective in various areas of your life. Perhaps you are a wonderful blessing to people in your community and an encourager of the brethren. The only problem is that you are continually defeated. You think just like Satan does. If you war with negative thoughts, feel discouraged all the time, or believe that you cannot live free from satanic control, then you think like the devil does. And the only way you will ever be free is when you come to the knowledge of God.

You probably know God as a loving Savior. That is how you received salvation. You may even know Him as a Healer, for that is how you received your healing. However you perceive God is how He will be to you. So if you have never seen God as a Warrior, you will never experience what it is actually like to have the all-powerful God working things out for you. You are regularly defeated in certain areas only because you don't realize that God can help you out in the areas that challenge you. Most people believe God is just a Savior, so that is what they get from Him: salvation. God is more than that—He is a Man of War. British Methodist theologian Adam Clarke wrote:

[The LORD is a man of war] Perhaps it would be better to translate the words, "Yahweh is the man or hero of the battle." As we scarcely ever apply the term to anything but first-rate armed vessels, the change of the translation seems indispensable, though the common rendering is literal enough. Besides, the object of Moses was to show that man had no part in this victory, but that the whole was wrought by the miraculous power of God, and that therefore he alone should have all the glory.[1]

God the Warrior wants an opportunity to fight for you. There is a time for you to fight and a time for you to refrain from fighting. God does not want to fight with you since He really does not need any help. And according to Adam Clarke, God won't chance giving you a piece of the action so as to clearly distinguish who's really worthy of the credit. You've been fighting for a long time now, and losing. It's time once and for all to ask for Yahweh's help. You cannot do it without Him.

A CLOSER LOOK AT OUR GOD OF WAR

When we talk about spiritual warfare, we are not just prancing around our favorite Charismatic songs, or our preferred power Scriptures, or our favorite ten confessions. You can sing spiritual warfare songs at the top of your lungs, and all that will do is summon the devil to sing along with you. It's much more than that. Spiritual warfare equates to fighting. In that fight two roles are being played: your role and God's role.

God's Role:

He who sins is of the devil, for the devil has sinned from the beginning. For this purpose the Son of God was manifested, that He might destroy the works of the devil (1 John 3:8).

The very reason Jesus came into the earthly realm is to combat and win against every evil, diabolical plan that the enemy has against your life's assignment. Jesus came to destroy the multitudinous works of darkness. Those are works that strive against every area of your life and your developmental growth process. So anything that hinders your ability to grow in a healthy manner in any area of your life can be viewed as an assignment from hell to stop you. And that's what Jesus came to destroy.

Your Role:

Fight the good fight of faith, lay hold on eternal life, to which you were also called and have confessed the good confession in the presence of many witnesses (1 Timothy 6:12).

Just because God is fighting for you does not mean that you are exempt from the warring process altogether. You too have a very specific role to play. So let's review. Your role and God's role are very different. He destroys the work of the devil; you and I lay hold of life through faith. You are obligated to fight the fight of faith. It's very interesting that our fight is called the *"fight of faith."* God's fight simply involves destroying the works of the devil. Hidden in First Timothy 6:12 is the notion that while you are in this warring, your faith will ultimately be challenged. It is in your best interest to keep the faith that you have, lest you lose it and be annihilated by the enemy.

Keep the faith, keep the goal in view, and keep confessing and praying. Those elements simplify your entire responsibility in this thing. That's the map for how to fight your fight. But is that all?

Well, there are some other things you will need as you go along. But those are the basics. After you have mastered those fundamental things, you should check out this much-needed Scripture:

> *For though we walk in the flesh, we do not war according to the flesh. For the weapons of our warfare are not carnal but mighty in God for pulling down strongholds, casting down arguments and every high thing that exalts itself against the knowledge of God, bringing every thought into captivity to the obedience of Christ, and being ready to punish all disobedience when your obedience is fulfilled* (2 Corinthians 10:3-6).

Since the battle you will face is mostly waged in your mind, you must set up some ground rules for what you allow to go into your mind. Even the best security guards cannot always see the intruder. The United States government has perhaps one of the best secret service divisions in the world. But that was still not enough to prevent John Hinckley, Jr. from shooting a bullet into former President Ronald Reagan's flesh. My point is that things enter in. Sometimes we know how the thoughts got there, and sometimes we don't.

When you do your part, God can do His part.

The bottom line is that once they've arrived, you cannot welcome them and ask them to stick around for a while. You must immediately serve an eviction notice for them to quit the premises of your mind at once. How do you do this? You do this by *"casting down arguments and every high thing that exalts itself against the knowledge of God."* You have to become an expert at casting vain, unfruitful, ungodly, and unholy thoughts down before they can take good root in the soil of your mind.

When you do your part, you give God the leeway to go ahead and kill your enemy. It is sort of like clearing the fields for God so He can have a clear shot at the devil. The Scriptures are replete with verse after verse that describe God as a bold and courageous Deity ready and willing to defend His posterity. You may not have seen Him in this light before, but from this moment on you will see God for who He is. God is your Friend and an Opponent of your enemies.

WEAPON OF CHOICE

To end this chapter I would like to introduce you to God's weapon of choice. (We will deal with His choice of armaments for you later on.) God is essentially spirit. He does not have to protect His Spirit because His Spirit cannot be permeated by outside carnal forces. In other words, you cannot hurt God. You can't diminish Him. He is impervious to your attack. In the most foundational sense, you really can't attack God.

Years ago there was a movie called *The Last Temptation of Christ* that was aired around the country, whose undermining theme was to portray Christ in an unholy light. Many Christians immediately began to protest the movie, claiming that it was an attack against God. Although that may appear to be the case, it really doesn't make sense. You can only attack something of like value and substance. America can attack Iraq, since both Iraq and America are countries. A mugger can attack a victim, since they are both people. A wolf can attack a vulnerable sheep, since they are both animals. The Democrats can attack the Republicans, since they are both political parties. I hope you are you getting the point.

You cannot attack God because you are not big enough to do so. A better way of saying this is that you are not God enough to attack God. Only God could attack God because only God is in the same class with God. Since God is in a class by Himself, no one can defeat Him. So He does not protect His Spirit because it does not need protecting. And God only uses one method of weaponry that works every time. God uses the sword. You've heard the old adage, "If it ain't broke, why fix it?" The sword works every time.

What exactly is the sword? A sword is a knife-like or cutting weapon that a soldier would use to stab or lacerate his foe. Swords were made differently depending on the purpose. Some swords were designed to pierce; others were made to slash. The one thing that both types had in common was their composition: a handle or hilt and a razor-sharp blade. The blade was usually straight, but one unusual variation was the sickle sword, which was designed mainly for agricultural use. This weapon featured a curved blade with the sharp edge on the outside. Swords were the basic weapon of a Hebrew soldier.

In one sense the sword symbolically refers to the Word of God. Ephesians 6:17 says, *"And take the helmet of salvation, and the sword of the Spirit, which is the word of God."* But this is still from the believer's position. We need the Word of God as our weaponry. God doesn't need the Word because He is the Word. So the other symbolic application illustrates the sword as an instrument of war. It shows the sword utilized as a tool of judgment and as a weapon to slaughter the wicked.

Arise, O LORD, confront him, cast him down; deliver my life from the wicked with Your sword (Psalm 17:13).

It is time to take your rightful place as a believer and kingdom citizen. It's true that you are a solider in the army of the Lord. And yes, it is also true that you have to fight if you expect to stay on top. But the consoling truth is that you have the most remarkable Chief and Commanding Officer, the Lord Jesus Christ, over the army. He has designed this whole effort for you to win by employing *His* war tactics to defeat your enemy. The world uses violence; God uses peace. The world uses threats; you and I use prayer.

The world uses resistance; we use godly submission. God has intentionally given us a different kind of a strategy to defeat a diabolical assignment. I'm not concerned about how much I look like a soldier or how great my fighting skills appear to be. I just want to know beyond any doubt that when I obey God's command, as strange as it may be, that after the battle is over, I have won the war.

And the God of peace will crush Satan under your feet shortly. The grace of our Lord Jesus Christ be with you. Amen

(Romans 16:20).

Endnote

1. *Adam Clarke's Commentary*, Electronic Database. Copyright „ 1996 by Biblesoft.

CHAPTER TWO

UNDERSTANDING SPIRITUAL WARFARE

So many viewpoints vary on what spiritual warfare is and what it is not. Actually, the phrase *spiritual warfare* is never mentioned in the Scriptures. However, the whole concept of war and spiritual conflict is clearly seen throughout almost the entire Bible. In fact, the entire Bible can be viewed as a Book that helps people overcome spiritual conflicts by accessing the power of God. How we deal with our conflicts, or even whether we deal with them at all, is the center of spiritual warfare. And what you choose to ignore now does not go away in time, as some mistakenly believe. To the contrary, you *must* deal with it.

After all, will cancer or AIDS suddenly disappear simply because you deny that they exist? Of course not! That cancer or AIDS will only get worse if left untreated or ignored. This is often the state of the body of Christ. Although the body is very much alive and still accomplishing great things, it is very ill with a malady that it refuses to openly or inwardly acknowledge. As a result, slow decay is occurring. On the outside it may appear as if a particular church is thriving because it boasts 3,000-plus members. But that alone does not depict either its value or its present health condition.

It may appear that since a particular evangelist travels more than a quarter of a million miles each year, everything is running smoothly in his or her ministry. But the reality may be that while the evangelist's ministry is effectively advancing in the efforts to reach lost souls, which is what everyone on the outside sees, on the inside the ministry is carrying unprecedented amounts of debt and regularly breaking promises to its creditors. Little does the leader of the ministry realize that the battle is not a physical or even a fiscal one; it is a spiritual one. The constant cycle of debt is not a normal condition for any believer, and it should never be accepted as such.

Let's roll with that concept for a minute. Debt, as ordinary as it may be, is perhaps one of the top enemy agents warring against the body of Christ and ultimately limiting its potential to impact the world. The point is that we don't identify certain things as agents of war once we have become accustomed to them. That is the main strategy of spiritual warfare and spiritual conflict. The "thing" that is warring against you does not intend to fight you forever. That thing wants to become your family, or at least your good friend.

Why is that? Think about it. You would never have any reason to boot your friends or family members out of your house even if they had very annoying or intolerable traits. People who are close to you eventually become archived relics in your life. So it does not really matter how badly they behave; they get the privilege of still hanging out with you because they are family or they have become like family. It is the same way in the spiritual warfare arena. After the agents of the enemy have been inside you long enough, you adapt to them. They become like resident interns.

The problem is this: As friendly as they may appear to be, they are destructive and potently harmful. You must realize that the devil, no matter how he presents him or herself, came to steal, to kill, and to destroy. *"The thief does not come except to steal, and to kill, and to destroy. I have come that they may have life, and that they may have it more abundantly"* (John 10:10). At first the adversarial agents will not appear to be destructive. Instead they will stay within the soul of humanity for so long that it becomes their habitation. And when you least expect it, out of nowhere they strike and kill.

So what exactly is spiritual warfare?

SPIRITUAL WARFARE DEFINED

Spiritual warfare is essentially the art of warring against spiritual, non-material entities using God's power and wisdom to fight and conquer them.

If you think about spiritual warfare in the context of natural fighting of flesh against flesh, then you'll widely miss the point. It's not that at all. Every fight that you will fight in life, other than battles of spiritual warfare, is against targets that you can actually see. Every boxer can see an opponent right in front of him or her. Boxers know exactly how to punch at their target with great expectations of knocking the other person out. That's a real advantage. In spiritual warfare you know that your enemy is the devil; that's your advantage. However, you are not always certain where he resides or how to find him. Your target is invisible, which makes it very difficult for you to score against him.

You're swinging, yet never making contact. You are ducking, only to encounter a hard blow that rocks your whole being. It seems that no matter what you try to do to avoid confrontation, you find yourself in a worse position. The bottom line is that you must come face to face with what's ailing you spiritually if you ever want to have a fruitful and productive life.

IT'S ALL ABOUT CONFRONTING

One of the main things that most people cannot stand to do in life is confront. People may have terrible in-laws, disgruntled children, rude bosses, manipulative parents, non-supportive spouses, or even downright disrespectful siblings, yet they refuse to confront those people about the issues. The main reason people are so afraid to confront is that they feel that confrontation will cause friction and confusion and lead to a small war. Even I have to admit that is true. We try our level best to avoid war.

The problem is that war is inevitable. You will either enter the war now or enter it later; the choice is yours. Not confronting an issue does not mean that it will disappear. And spiritual warfare is all about confrontation. Now, before you run away with this idea and start feeling judgmental, hold on just a moment. Although people love to find the fault in others, *spiritual warfare begins with confronting your own self.* It begins with confronting the things in your life that you've ignored, that have either gotten out of control or are on their way to being totally out of control. Clean up your own mess before trying to clean up someone else's!

Spiritual warfare begins with confronting your own self.

One of the most dangerous things I've ever seen is when a person begins to confront another person's war when the first person has not dealt with his or her own. You cannot effectively war for another person until you've first battled and won on your own behalf. Perhaps I just destroyed your theology with that statement. Or maybe I've dampened your aggressive attitude about "helping" others in their spiritually declining states. Believe me when I tell you that I am not trying to do either. What I am intentionally trying to do is save your life. *You may never have been told this before, but spiritual warfare is not for novices.* It is only for those who have enlisted in God's army and who are totally sold out to the purposes of the kingdom of God.

Anyone can enlist, but not everyone will last. Those who are destroyed the quickest are those who had no idea what they were getting into and rushed into battle, only to discover that they were not properly armed or armored. Spiritual warfare is just what it sounds like; it's a spiritual war. You must be trained spiritually in order to win this war. I've seen so many ministers, pastors, leaders, and laypersons get slaughtered by the devil over the years. The main reason they were defeated is that they tried to use their intellectual acumen to defeat the devil.

Believe it or not, the enemy has more degrees than most people will ever dream of having. So you graduated from seminary or Bible college. Does that make you qualified to confront the spirits of darkness? I sure hope you do not think so. I too have graduated from seminary and Bible college. I'm a firm believer in education. However, I am fully aware of its limitations. I know what it can and cannot do. Good Bible school training will help me make wise choices if I apply what I've learned to my everyday life. It will also help me get a pastoral position in a mainline church that is seeking a pastor.

With that education I could teach at a university or a Bible school. Such training can be lucrative and fulfilling. However, when it comes to confronting age-old demons, I am not convinced that your schooling is going to help you. One thing that is not taught in seminary is how to confront the devil. And confronting the works of the devil is the whole essence of spiritual warfare. Preparation should always precede engagement. Going to battle without the proper training is absolutely perilous, yet many people do it all the time.

Have you ever heard of a Navy Seal becoming a Seal without first going through the prescribed training? I'm sure you have not. You may have been the captain of your high school swim team, but that does not qualify you to be a Navy Seal. You may love beaches and lakes, but that doesn't afford you the high privilege of being called a Navy Seal either. You have to go through the training so that when you come into confrontation you will know exactly how to respond, or if you should refrain from responding altogether.

Being a Navy veteran myself, I have always been interested in exactly what Navy Seals go through in their training regimen. It was very interesting to read of their workout, their dietary requirements, and the mental toughness needed for the job, and also to learn that the trainees could possibly die during their preliminary training. It would take up too much space if I were to list everything mentioned on their website as it relates to their training. (You can read the full list on their website at www.navyseals.com.)

Hopefully you are getting the point: Preparation precedes winning a confrontation both in the spiritual and the natural. You need to be prepared!

KNOW YOUR ENEMY

Speaking spiritually, a confrontation occurs in three stages. First you have to locate your enemy. It is quite obvious that you cannot confront what you cannot identify. Too often Christians label everything as the devil. Although the devil is the prince of darkness, he cannot take full credit for every dark situation that happens in your life.

If you were to be brutally honest, you'd have to admit that some things you've experienced in life you brought on yourself. In fact, in many instances you may have been warned over and over again not to enter into this or that situation. Despite the warnings, you still chose to involve yourself in areas that were charted as dangerous territory. Once you arrived at that place, you realized that what everyone was saying was really true. Then you started crying, "Devil!" I am like Jesus in that I too am here to destroy the works of the devil; so I'm not taking up for the devil at all. But I want you to know that not everything is the devil's work. Some things come about as a result of our own ignorance, rebellion, and disobedience.

Some people got married in ignorance, rebellion, and disobedience. Others started businesses stemming from ignorance, rebellion, and disobedience. We cannot even count the number of churches around the world that were organized as a direct result of ignorance, rebellion, and disobedience. Children were born into the world as a result of ignorance, rebellion, and disobedience. I personally know people who have lost all their life's savings by making bad investments based on ignorance, rebellion, and disobedience. The list can go on and on. You must see that when anything is a result of ignorance, rebellion, and disobedience, it is bound to fail. And when it does it's not the devil's fault, but rather your own.

So first identify your enemy. You have to know that the attack really is coming from the devil and is not an attack against you by yourself. So many people fail to properly grasp this concept. They find themselves fighting a senseless fight, never realizing that they are fighting against themselves...and winning. It wasn't the devil that got you into that trouble; it was your own ignorance, rebellion, and disobedience. Once you confess that as sin, you'll be grounded to move forward. Know who your enemy is.

KNOW YOUR TOOLS

The next thing you have to know is what tool to use against the enemy. A farmer must know what tool to use in order to produce abundant crops year after year. If he used a plow to turn under the existing crops ready to be harvested, within minutes he would have wasted an entire season of preparing for his harvest. The plow is not the proper tool for harvesting. It is used to prepare the soil for the seed. It cultivates the soil by separating the rocks and stone from the dirt so the seed will have pure soil to attach itself to.

Just as a good farmer knows exactly what tool to use and when to use it, so in spiritual warfare you have to know exactly what tool to cast against the devil. Some tools work some of the time for certain situations. You have to discern by the spirit—and properly discerning takes time and perseverance—exactly what tool to use and when you should use it. There are three primary tools used in spiritual warfare: prayer, praise, and sowing seeds. Each of these tools is extremely effective in defeating the enemy. But you need to know the right time to use them.

For example, you shouldn't sow a seed if the soil is not conducive to growth. No matter how many seeds you sow, you'll never reap a harvest if the soil is contaminated. Also, you have to understand the times and season for sowing. Even though it is good to sow all the time, there are some specific times that are better for sowing than other times. It's the same with prayer and praise. The Bible says in First Thessalonians 5:17, *"Pray without ceasing."*

Now, don't be mistaken. That Scripture is not suggesting that you and I should pray out loud continuously. Rather, it is saying that we should never be caught without a prayer in our hearts. The inward prayer is a continuous one for the believer. It never ceases to make intercession. Much like your brain still functions even while you are asleep, the prayer of the soul continues to communicate with God even when you don't realize it. It functions automatically. But if you and I were to pray out loud all the time, not only would it be greatly annoying to everyone around us, but it also would give the devil your exact location, assisting him in carrying out your own demise.

I'll deal with these weapons in greater detail later on in the book. So for now, just realize that you have to employ certain tools to defeat your enemy, and you need to know which one to use and when.

Although I've listed three primary tools that you should use, I must mention another posture that will help you to be effective in spiritual warfare. I'm not so sure that it can really be labeled as a tool. I do know that, regardless of how it is labeled, it works time after time. I am talking about the place or position of silence. The Bible has this to say:

Be still, and know that I am God; I will be exalted among

the nations, I will be exalted in the earth! (Psalm 46:10)

You have to know when to be heard from and when to remain in silence. In the Book of Judges, Gideon's army of 300 men won the battle against the Midianites using this same method. They knew when to be silent and when to blow their trumpets, letting the enemy know of their divine backing. Had they sounded off the trumpets too soon, they would have spoiled the surprise and given the victory into the hands of their adversary.

> *And he said to them, "Look at me and do likewise; watch, and when I come to the edge of the camp you shall do as I do: when I blow the trumpet, I and all who are with me, then you also blow the trumpets on every side of the whole camp, and say, 'The sword of the LORD and of Gideon!' "* (Judges 7:17-18)

Much of spiritual warfare is tightly wrapped in spiritual timing. When you are silent, you are able to hear directives given by the King. When you are silent, you are becoming at peace with yourself and ultimately at peace with your God. Most of all, you will be able to learn everything that you should because your listening and discerning skills are being developed as you remain silent.

Spiritual timing is key to spiritual warfare.

A good student listens in class and takes both written and mental notes. When the time for examination comes, the good students pass the exam with flying colors. When it was time to listen, they listened well. They kept silent. The ones who talked during the class lectures failed the test. They were not quiet at the appropriate time, and it cost them greatly. "To speak or not to speak, that is the question." And the answer to that question is that there is a time and place for everything, a time to speak and a time to refrain from speaking altogether.

KNOW WHEN TO CONFRONT

Finally, you have to know when to confront and when not to confront. That is crucial! If you act at the wrong time, the enemy may very well blow you to smithereens. There are times, many times, when you should confront. But there are other times when you should simply wait. Some spiritual situations God wants to confront on His own. If you choose to confront at the wrong time, you may avert His plans.

Spiritual warfare is not like natural warfare. In natural warfare you may or may not confront a serious situation based on your shyness or timidity. Spiritual warfare is not personality-based. You may be the shyest person in the world, yet be filled with power when it comes to defeating the devil. It's all about your stratagem. You can only overcome the devil's plan when you come to recognize and realize his tactics and know what to do to overcome them.

GETTING IN THE RIGHT POSITION

Position is everything when you are attempting to conquer the enemy. In nearly every competitive sport, positioning usually gives a team the advantage. Spiritual warfare is all about proper positioning. Where are you standing? Are you standing in a position where you are praying with the authority of God, or are you in a position where you are trying to pray through to God, having to permeate the satanic region in order to break through to God's throne room?

You may ask why this is so important. I have a question to pose to you first. Suppose you are playing a competitive sport where you can score points on the offensive side, such as basketball, soccer, football, lacrosse or baseball. Let's say that the person with the ball is running toward the goal, intending to score a point against the defending team. Do you think that the defending team players would stand by and let the person score without trying to stop him or her? I'm sure you know that they would not.

Secondly, do you really believe that each team member on the defense would stand in the same place close together, talking and jesting, while the other team runs toward victory? It would be highly improbable for that to happen. Each team member has to be in the right position to defend the team against the opponent as well as to score against the other team. Being in the wrong position could very well cost them the entire game.

Much of the body of Christ has been in a loser's position. We have condescended to the low level of feeling comfortable about the devil's advances and triumphs over us. And one of the main reasons the enemy is victorious is that we are, for the most part, out of place. We do not understand spiritual placement. As a result, we are continually being destroyed because of what we don't know. Hosea comments on the same spiritually deficient condition:

> *My people are destroyed for lack of knowledge. Because you have rejected knowledge, I also will reject you from being priest for Me; because you have forgotten the law of your God, I also will forget your children* (Hosea 4:6).

So then, what position should the believer take when doing battle? As any good soldier knows, your positioning is totally contingent upon the situation at hand. There are times when it is best to kneel. At other times the soldier must lie down in a prostrate position. When engaged with gunfire, the soldier must be in a position to destroy the enemy with his ammunition. Thus the answer is that it really depends on the situation and on what the Holy Spirit is calling for at the moment.

Some people in Christian circles falsely believe that the permanent position for the believer should be on his or her knees. That may sound really spiritual, but that is just not using spiritual sense. There is a time to pray out loud, to intercede, and of course to fast. But that time is not all of the time. There are so many people who use prayer and fasting as an excuse to escape from the responsibilities of engagement. When it's time to fight, it's time to fight.

I once heard an old preacher say, "You don't pray in a bear meeting: You run." Prayer is a preparatory working. Much like taking multivitamins, getting proper and adequate exercise, and drinking plenty of purified water, prayer is a preventative mechanism. When you have already prayed, you will be able to defeat the devil. But if you have not prayed, then when the devil comes face to face with you, I'd advise you to run quickly.

If you have not already prepared yourself ahead of time, he will inevitably defeat you. We'll also discuss later the fact that you need to know how to pray. In other words, you need to know how to position yourself spiritually so that every prayer you pray will be a victorious one. Perhaps you did not know that you are capable of having never-ending prayer success. You should never be defeated in prayer—if you know how to do it. I will show you exactly how to do that. Once you've mastered the knowledge, you'll not only win in prayer, but you also will win when engaged in warfare, time after time.

THE BATTLE IS ALL IN YOUR MIND

One other thing I want you to know is that the battle is all in your mind. To properly understand spiritual warfare, you must recognize that the battle you are facing is not an external battle. The battle is very close to you; it is very much internal. It is in your mind, your soulish realm. That is exactly where all the combat happens. Unfortunately, the church at large has falsely taught its followers that our problems as well as our adversary are personal things. That is a lie. It's a lie that the devil wants you to continually buy into so that you will never confront the real enemy.

Despite what your mother or father did or did not do for you as child, or even how horribly they treated you, you can outlive their low expectations of you and their abuses if you will conquer those self-defeating thoughts in your mind. If the enemy conquers your mind, he'll never need to attack your flesh. He doesn't have authority to touch your spirit because that area is sacred territory, reserved only for God. So the only way he can enter into your spirit is through contaminating your mind—with your express permission.

I've heard many preachers call the devil dumb and ignorant. Now, I'm not here to proclaim him a genius or a Rhodes Scholar, but one thing I do know is that he is a master planner. He is a great strategist, and he is very systematic at following through on his carefully mapped-out plan. Celebrated author and teacher Joyce Meyer writes this regarding this topic:

> He begins by bombarding our mind with a cleverly devised pattern of little nagging thoughts, suspicions, doubts, fears, wonderings, reasonings and theories. He moves slowly and cautiously (after all, well laid plans take time). Remember, he has a strategy for his warfare. He has studied us for a long time.
>
> He knows what we like and what we don't like. He knows our insecurities, our weaknesses and our fears. He knows what bothers us most. He is willing to invest any amount of time it takes to defeat us. One of the devil's strong points is patience.[1]

Sometimes I wonder how effective the church of the Lord Jesus Christ would actually be if we exercised the same discipline, planning, and patience as the devil does. By now we would surely have summoned the return of Christ the King! Sadly, we have fallen short in the area of discipline. Most Christians are not disciplined in any area of their lives. Many of us have major challenges with immoral thoughts, perverted behavioral patterns, overeating, overspending, and gossiping and slandering other fellow believers with our tongues.

Many parishioners are not even disciplined enough to attend church regularly, pay tithes and offerings, and faithfully pray for their spiritual leaders and their families. It is this lack of discipline that invites the devil into the thought patterns of humankind. Once there, he has a field day wreaking havoc in this fresh new territory. The truth is that the devil will have a very difficult time scoring in the life of the disciplined believer.

I am not trying to make you feel condemned. Condemnation is a work of the devil. *"There is therefore now no condemnation to those who are in Christ Jesus, who do not walk according to the flesh, but according to the Spirit"* (Romans 8:1). I'm just trying to convey to you the reason the enemy attacks you and the method he usually uses. If you can protect your mind from demonic influences, you will have far more victories than you've ever imagined.

Living close to our nation's capital, I can't help but be influenced by and notice the tightness in our national security, particularly in the White House. Prior to the tragic terrorist attacks on our nation on that dreadful day, September 11, 2001, millions of people were able to freely visit the White House, the oldest standing house in Washington, D.C. where most of our presidents lived, worked, and gave their famous speeches. Because of the attack, our security had to be tightly increased. Although the terrorist attack never actually hit the White House, but rather destroyed the Twin Towers at the World Trade Center in New York City and damaged the Pentagon in Virginia, our national security used that as a warning to protect our prized presidential home with even greater intensity. The lesson is that you don't have to have things happen directly to you in order to benefit from the message. You can learn from other people's

Protect your mind from demonic influences and you will have more victories than you've ever imagined

experiences vicariously.

Today, in order for Americans to get a tour of the White House, we must write a letter to our Congressional representative, depending on which state we reside in, requesting a private visit of the White House. We have to give them the dates when we intend to travel. And we have to give them at least a six-months' window in which to respond. There are no more quickie, unplanned visits. They need to know about the applicant's background in advance before entry is granted. They cannot chance the possibility of allowing total strangers to freely roam around in this territory. The house is extremely valuable. So every request is carefully recorded.

They want to know who is coming in and who is going out. Our government realizes that when something is highly valuable, you must guard it with all diligence. It's the same with the mind. Your mind is extremely valuable. In fact, it is priceless. Before anyone can be allowed to get into your mind or to have access to your mind, they ought to have to first apply and go through a screening process. You need to have the privilege of rejecting or accepting requests based on your highly discriminating process of acceptance.

When you begin to view your mind as sacred territory that only a select few can access, you will greatly minimize the attacks of the devil against you. Your mind is what the enemy is after. It's what he lusts for. It is the only place where he can successfully wage war. Close him out of your mind. Make it known to him that your mind will no longer be a territory he is allowed to use, even for a short amount of time. If he can't use your mind, he'll be forced to move on to the next vulnerable victim. Make sure that he can't victimize you anymore! Say this out loud right now:

"Devil, you cannot have my mind, you cannot lease my mind, and you cannot wage war in my mind. I won't allow it ever again. I now realize that if I stop you from accessing my mind, you won't have anywhere to wage

war and perform your day-to-day activities. My mind belongs to God, and if you ever enter this region, you'll be trespassing on sovereign territory. If you should ever be found intruding in my mind, you'll be forced out using the most lethal weapons that I can use. Stay away from me and everything that pertains to my life. In Jesus' name. Amen."

For "who has known the mind of the LORD that he may instruct Him?" But we have the mind of Christ
(1 Corinthians 2:16).

Endnote

1. Joyce Meyer, *Battlefield of the Mind: Winning the Battle in Your Mind* (Tulsa, Oklahoma: Harrison House, 1995), pp. 15-16.

CHAPTER THREE

FIGHTING THE GOOD FIGHT

When I hear the fighting phrase, *good fight*, I immediately know that in order to have a good fight there must also be a bad fight. The very concept of evil could never exist if there was not good to differentiate itself from it. So, I know from hearing this phrase that there is a right way and a wrong way of fighting. That goes for any kind of fight. In boxing there are coaches who train their fighters to properly fight so as to last all ten rounds, so they can still stand after sustaining repeated blows to the body.

There are certain things they can do while fighting that will cause major injury to themselves. Those things they must avoid at all costs. There are other things that, done properly, will cause them to last and win the fight with seemingly little effort. A good coach will teach their boxers exactly what it is they need to know. For far too long now, the body of Christ has been fighting the bad fight, having no coach to follow. You may think that sounds a bit harsh. You may also wonder exactly how I came to such a conclusion.

It's really simple. Any fight that you lose as a believer is a bad fight. It's as simple as that. God has not called us to lose any battles. He has called us to win every single time. So the good fight can be defined as the fight that we win. That is the fight Christ expects us to engage in. Any other fight is a waste of precious time.

Do you think that a professional boxer goes into the ring with the expectations of nearly getting beaten to death by his or her opponent? Absolutely not! The fighter should always believe deep down within that he or she will come out the victor. To think anything less could be fatal. And if you have been properly trained as a fighter, you usually walk into the ring with a fresh confidence that you will win by employing the skills you've rehearsed over and over till they are second nature.

TO LOSE OR NOT TO LOSE

I've already dealt with the concept of preparation and how every believer seriously needs to be prepared before going into battle. But something equally as important as preparation to win is the attitude that we have concerning loss. Many believers have become so accustomed to losing in every area of their lives that it is now normal for them. That's totally crazy; it's insane. But unfortunately it's just the way that it has become. It is also one of the main reasons many are defeated in warfare.

Unbelievers and pagans often have a more optimistic outlook on life than Christians do. Many unbelievers consciously expect to have money and plenty of it. They expect their children to grow up in a healthy environment, attend the finest schools, finish college, and then marry their dream spouse and start the same cycle of rearing children all over again. They expect that. They expect to work for the best companies, earn the highest salaries, or maybe even own the company altogether. They expect to go on regular vacations to wherever they want to go, enjoying the very best that life has to offer.

Now, I am not trying to suggest that they always have their wishes manifested 100 percent of the time. You and I both know that some win and some lose in life. That's just the name of the game. But more often than not, I've seen people winning over and over again, particularly when they have the right attitude concerning how they want to live out their lives. It's not just about having a P.M.A (Positive Mental Attitude) or saying confessions or repeating ritualistic mantras. It's far more than that.

It's about knowing who you are in Christ. Once you know who you are, all your expectations then begin to revolve around your knowledge of who you are. So then, when you know that you are rich because Christ became poor so that you could become rich in every way, you then begin to act on what you know. You begin to behave as you *It's all about knowing who you are in Christ.* know you ought to behave, based on the expected actions of your inner character.

I've heard Christians say things that immediately caused them to lose their battle in life, such as, "My child is on his way to jail." Or, "My son will never get out of jail." They say things like that in the first place because jail and juvenile imprisonment are comfortable parts of their reality. For other parents whose thoughts are far more elevated, prison is not even an option for them or anyone remotely related to them.

When the thought of something is not even an option for you, then the fruits of that thought can never conquer you in battle because they do not have a chance to materialize. On the other hand, you'll consistently lose battles in spiritual warfare when you fight with preconceived notions that the evil before you actually belongs in your life.

Think about it. How often do we become satisfied with death, even premature death? We make statements such as, "Everybody has got to die at some time or another." When referring to a young person who has passed away far too prematurely, I've heard people say, "Well, God knows best. He must have had reason to take my child away." Ridiculous statements such as this only indicate how you think. You can only utter thoughts that are within you. Thoughts just don't appear out of nowhere; they come from within. They are solidified through daily meditation and constant rehearsing. That is the main reason the Scriptures command us to cast down vain imaginations, which are unproductive thoughts.

If you don't cast them down, they will ultimately destroy you. Poverty, sickness and disease, divorce, repeated failure, and emotional instability are all attacks from the enemy. You need to realize that the enemy cannot win while fighting against you unless you have made those negative things a reality in your life, in your mind. So while it's true that you can win the battle against the adversary every time, that will only happen when you begin to surrender your thoughts to Christ's thoughts. It will happen when you choose once and for all to stop helping the devil whip on you by lending him your negative realities. Despite how intense your warfare may become, always remember that you are not a loser. You are designed to win!

For as he thinks in his heart, so is he. "Eat and drink!" he says to you, but his heart is not with you (Proverbs 23:7).

DON'T PLAY FAIR

One thing that people seem to demand in a free society is justice and equity. Everybody wants to be treated with respect and to be valued. Although the ethic of equity should be a standard for all of humanity, and especially for believers, every believing soul must draw the line when it comes to confronting the spirits of darkness. You cannot afford to try to play fairly when it comes to the devil. The devil never, ever plays fair. If he can kill you, he will. He will destroy you, given the right opportunity. As believers, our warfare is always a spiritual one.

We don't fight the enemy using the same methods that he uses against us. If you try to use the same method that the devil uses, you will be defeated. Why? For one reason, the devil has been using his devices for so long that he has become a skilled expert at doing what he does. Imagine your average basketball enthusiast trying to compete against Michael Jordan, Dwayne Wade, Kobe Bryant, or LeBron James. That amateur would be bound for failure before the game even started. All those professional players are highly skilled at what they do. In order to defeat them, you would have to discover totally new ways of playing the game of basketball, ways with which they are unfamiliar.

The devil has a great sensitivity to things that are familiar. And he has great ability to master those things that he has used for millennia. So if you truly desire to defeat the devil—and you can—you must use a method that he has not conquered. It is not so much that our methods are completely foreign to the enemy. There are many great women and men of God from yesteryear and even today who have conquered Satan in battle many times. The thing that bothers him is that he has never been able to replicate our strategy. Our methods are different, but both the devil and we are equally committed to seeing the other one totally annihilated.

Growing up in north Jersey in the inner city, I was exposed to a whole lot of different kinds of kids. Although few existed, I knew the peacemakers. I also knew the mouthy troublemakers—the ones always inciting problems and using their big mouths to gas the fire of the already existing conflict. I also knew the big bullies—the overgrown, overfed kids who were twice the size of my friends, who always used their big size to push and shove the other kids at will. They, of course, did not need the provocation of the neighborhood troublemakers to provoke them. No, they were self-starters. Much like Satan, they were always running to and fro around the earth seeking out someone to devour.

I clearly remember when fights would break out in the neighborhood, the kids would all surround the two contenders with great anticipation of getting the best spot on the corner to view the showdown. Realizing that they had an enthusiastic crowd, both opponents recognized that the battle was viewed by a host of acquaintances and that they would have to do whatever it took to win. I'd often watch a big bully take such advantage of the guy with the frail little frame. Mr. Bully would take major potshots at the weak guy, knowing that he did not have the size, speed, or strength to defeat him.

Knowing that, the little guy would have to resort to any means necessary to survive, let alone win the fight. Just looking at the fight from an outsider's perspective, the bully was already at an advantage, and unfair to his opponent from the very start. He would take hard shots at the little guy, although he knew that much softer blows would have subdued his subject just as easily. Every now and then, though, the bully would be in for a rude awakening when his weakly challenger mustered up enough courage to fight back. The little guy could never compete using skillful punches, blocks, or throws. Not at all.

Rather, he would use any object nearby as a weapon to defend himself. That object could be a broken vodka bottle, a torn-open soda can, a brick, the lid of a trash can, a sharp knife, a rope, or whatever deterrent he could find. From out of nowhere we'd see blood and bruising; an old-fashioned whipping on the big old bully. The little guy would suddenly realize that he could overcome his enemy if he used weapons that were totally unexpected.

The occasional punch or kick just would not do. In order to defeat this bully he'd have to get outright unfair—violent, in fact. Not only would the little guy win the victory, but he would also cause the neighborhood bully to think twice before ever engaging in a battle with him again. When fighting the devil, you cannot be fair. You have got to go for the kill immediately. If you don't, he will. And you will not only lose, but also possibly die in the process.

One good thing about this whole situation is that you are not the little kid in the example. In fact, you are greater than any devil since Jesus lives inside you. *"You are of God, little children, and have overcome them, because He who is in you is greater than he who is in the world"* (1 John 4:4). If the Greater One lives inside you, that devil is in no position to bully you. In fact, you are in the position to bully him, although you may not have realized it yet.

So the devil really is afraid of you. He is afraid that you may suddenly come into the knowledge of your truest self. He recognizes that once you discover the power within you and the weapons of your warfare, you will no longer be intimidated by his unfair moves. One strong blow to the devil's weak spot will take him out for good. You must know that. My friends never played fair because they knew what they were up against. You can't become friends with the devil. He will stab you in the back every single time. He will act as if he is your friend, but his ultimate intention is to kill you when he gets the right opportunity and the right positioning.

The devil really is afraid of you!

One of the ways in which I deal with the enemy is by intentionally trying to be as unfair as I can and nipping things in the bud as they arise. That may sound a bit overreactive, but one of the problems many Christians face is that they give too much allowance to the enemy, whether it is in the area of health, finance, unhealthy relationships, or poor character. I'm sure that you've heard it said, "If you give him an inch, he'll take a mile." The devil has to be shut down the very moment he tries to suggest a sinful thought or action to you. If you wait any later than that, he'll overcome you with evil.

Realize that sinfulness is not limited to our lists of sins that we have committed to memory; it extends far beyond that. Sin in God's eyes is missing His mark. Even if you come close to the target, by simply missing the mark by one inch you've sinned, according to God. I'm sure you are looking at this issue from a different perspective now. James gave perhaps the most conclusive definition:

> *Therefore, to him who knows to do good and does not do it, to him it is sin* (James 4:17).

So what good should you practice daily? You must practice the good of not giving any place to the devil. It does not matter whether that place is in the area of your thoughts, your actions, or even your motives and intentions; you must not give the devil place in your life. People may think you are always on the edge, always inferring things. But the truth is that it is better to be thought of as a bit strange while winning, than to be thought of as a normal loser. Do as Jesus did and you will have continuous victory, destroying the works of the devil.

> *Leave no [such] room or foothold for the devil [give no opportunity to him]* (Ephesians 4:27, AMP).

> There are only five notes in the musical scale, but their variations are so many that they cannot all be heard. There are only five basic colors, but their variations are so many that cannot all be seen. There are only five basic flavors, but their variations are so many that they cannot all be tasted. There are only two kinds of charge in battle, the unorthodox surprise attack and the orthodox direct attack, but variations of the unorthodox and orthodox are endless. The unorthodox and the orthodox give rise to each other, like a beginningless circle—who could exhaust them?

> — Master Sun

Never give the devil what he expects of you. Always surprise him with a new strategy that you discovered while praying and meditating in the presence of the Lord. Whether your tactics are orthodox or unorthodox, make sure that they accomplish your intended goal of defeating the devil in every way. When it came to the devil, Jesus never played fair, and neither should you. Surprise the devil. Get him when he is not expecting it. Don't give him notice. Treat him the same way that he'd treat you.

> *He who sins is of the devil, for the devil has sinned from the beginning. For this purpose the Son of God was manifested, that He might destroy the works of the devil* (1 John 3:8).

WHO ARE YOU FIGHTING, ANYWAY?

I would be negligent if I ended this chapter without discussing our adversary. Although I really do not like to talk about the devil too much, as it gives unnecessary attention to him, I still must deal with his nature for identity's sake. A very large reason our fight against the devil is so ineffectual is that we don't, for the most part, even fight the devil. In most cases we fight against everything except the devil. And that is precisely what he wants you to do.

The power of movies—you know, the big screen and television—is absolutely amazing. The movies that are produced today portray an image of the devil that is so far from reality that it is saddening. Worse yet is that most believers take their cues from movies and the media rather than from the Spirit of the Lord and His Word. The images that we conjure up in our minds are directly connected to the things that we have seen over the years that have subliminally spoon-fed our minds without our knowing it.

Most people automatically perceive the devil as a red, double-hoofed, animalistic creature with two sharp horns protruding from the top of his skull. And, of course, he has a red-hot pitchfork in his right hand to match his reddish exterior. This same ghastly-looking creature jumps nearly 20 feet high into the air, at times leaps over buildings, and always destroys things wherever he shows up. Most of his victims are terrified at his very sight. And that is the problem with many believers. They are looking for a devil that they can visibly identify, somewhat like the guy in the movies.

The sad truth is that the enemy wants you to continue to look at those images so that you can misidentify him in a lineup. If you try to combat the evil that looks like the red guy in the pictures, you'll never come face to face with confronting your greatest evil, which may be far closer to you than you first thought. I think it is important to find out a little bit of his history if we are going to engage in warfare against this nemesis. Far too many Christians live in ignorance. And it is that same ignorance that ultimately destroys them and their life's purpose. So we are going to break the spirit of ignorance right now in the mighty name of the Lord Jesus Christ.

Who exactly is the devil? The devil is the supreme spirit of all evil. He is the tempter of mankind and an adversary of God. Interestingly, he is still subordinate to God and cannot act without God's authority. What's more powerful is that he cannot do anything at all in the life of a believer without the express consent of the believer. The only way he can enter into the life of a believer is by private invitation. Although it is his innate nature to lure and tempt, ultimately he is unable to perform his work without sanction.

Because of the multitudinous work of the devil, he has been given several names. But before we go into the names and definitions, let me caution you that the devil is neither a he nor a she. For the sake of grammatical flow I have chosen to use "he" repeatedly to refer to the devil. This is not a gender-related or sexual orientation. It is only used as a common and understood approach for your reading ease. The reason I've chosen to mention this feature is because many people play the sexes against each other. However, there are no genders in the spirit world. So the devil is just as likely to show up in a male as a female or in a child or an adult. Stay focused on identifying the spirit, not the gender.

For example, so many people throughout my church journey have referred to Jezebel in Scripture. Jezebel was a native Zidonian, the daughter of Ethbaal and wife of Ahab the king of Israel, which made her a queen. Her most offensive evils were openly practicing idolatry and literally killing the prophets of God. *"Was it not reported to my lord what I did when Jezebel killed the prophets of the LORD, how I hid one hundred men of the LORD's prophets, fifty to a cave, and fed them with bread and water?"* (1 Kings 18:13) She was a wicked woman who even went so far as to make a vow to have the prophet Elijah murdered because of his allegiance to God and His servants.

It's obvious that this woman had a heavy-duty evil spirit. However, the majority of preachers I've heard who have referred to Jezebel immediately deduce her influence to be one of sexual seduction through the wearing of costly jewelry, cosmetics, and alluring and revealing clothing. Not only is this concept a false one, it is exactly the image that the enemy wants you and me to picture Jezebel as. If you look upon a woman who is sharply dressed, wearing fine perfume, whose makeup is impeccably applied, you may at first believe that she is an evil person…if that is what your limited knowledge will afford you.

You will make a misjudgment based on external evidences that are false, not realizing that the problem with Jezebel both then and now rests in her spirit, not her outward appearance. A woman can be fully clothed, makeup-free, wearing a long dress with a turban on her head, yet have a very strong Jezebel spirit within her. The undiscerning person will automatically fall for her outward appearance and buy into the cover-up. But that itself is gross deception. When you look at the outward to determine the potency of a spirit, you will lose the fight.

When you look at the outward, you will lose the fight.

However, when you recognize that a spirit is invisible and cannot be seen with the naked eye, then you will come into the knowledge of how damaging spirits can potentially be. Although Jezebel was a female and a queen, the spirit that she possessed was not limited to females. Rather, it can easily infect the unguarded soul. As I mentioned earlier, her passion was to kill off the prophets of God. So then anyone who opposes God's set authorities and tries to usurp authority over them has the spirit of Jezebel.

Anyone who does not regard spiritual authority as being a God-ordained delegation is operating under the influence of this Jezebel spirit. I've seen pastors' wives who usurp authority over their own husbands, neither submitting to them as their pastor nor as their husband. There have been cases when a pastor's wife got up in front of the congregation and made verbal threats toward the pastor, so as to have power over him. In other instances the pastor's wife was a whole lot more subtle and less obvious. She would simply wait until she got home before she started whirling off threats and ultimatums.

Regardless of where she made her demands, such a person was operating under a demonic spirit of Jezebel. There have been women who literally forced their husbands into making them assistant pastors and co-pastors, threatening that if they did not the wives would leave the church and disgrace the ministry. No matter how you look at it, it is outright unspiritual and ungodly. So outward appearance does not matter at all; it's what is going on the inside that counts most.

In the same way, the devil is a spirit. So the spirit of the devil has to find someone to dwell in, in order to have movement and free access. Again, it is not the outward appearance that matters, but rather the fruit people produce that will determine who they really are and to whom they belong. Jesus dealt with this same issue:

> *For a good tree does not bear bad fruit, nor does a bad tree bear good fruit. For every tree is known by its own fruit. For men do not gather figs from thorns, nor do they gather grapes from a bramble bush. A good man out of the good treasure of his heart brings forth good; and an evil man out of the evil treasure of his*

heart brings forth evil. For out of the abundance of the heart his mouth speaks (Luke 6:43-45).

It is rather interesting to note that after Jesus gave this short discourse on bearing good fruit as a sign of what is inside the heart of man, He did not speak one word about outward apparel. If the outward mattered most to our Lord, this would have been a primary opportunity to deal with that topic. Instead Jesus ended this dialogue saying, *"For out of the abundance of the heart his mouth speaks."* Jesus recognized the oft-forgotten truth that what is in you has to come out of you at some point. You will inevitably speak your beliefs and convictions. Those kinds of things you cannot hide, no matter how much you dress it up.

So you cannot be deceived any more from this moment on. The devil that you fight is not a Hollywood actor, but rather a very real spiritual entity that will oppose every progressive step you contemplate. In order to win this fight, you must realize who he is and know that he always travels in disguise. These disguises may have worked to fool the very elect of God in past times, but not now. You are not fighting a person, a denomination, a church, a pastor, a family member, or a friend. You are fighting a very real spirit who has many names and various functions, yet one very clear threefold objective: to steal, to kill, and to destroy. Know this!

WINNING THE BATTLE AGAINST...

The Bible gives many different labels for the devil. In the final analysis, the devil is still the devil. He is still wicked and evil and will ultimately be destroyed once the believer embraces the knowledge of God concerning his or her victorious warfare. A pig is called many things. Some call a pig a sow; others call a pig a boar or a hog. To the hungry individual a pig is called pork chops, pork roast, bacon, pastrami, or even a hot dog. Whether you call a pig dinner, breakfast, lunch, or the family pet, it's still a pig. The only reason you need to know when to call it a particular thing is to understand how to deal with that pig under certain conditions.

If a pig is uncooked, it could kill the person trying to consume it. Similarly, not knowing the function of the devil may cause the believer to give an unwarranted allowance to the devil that could be fatal. So in order to win the battle against the devil, we have to look past his disguise.

Mike Tyson, Trevor Berbick, Evander Holyfield, and Lennox Lewis are all boxers, yet they are very uniquely different. If you plan to defeat any one of these men in a fight, you will have to know what each person is capable of. That is why I thought it was necessary to provide you with a list of titles of the devil, giving the corresponding Scriptures. When you pray you need to be able to confront the spirits of darkness by name. Each demon spirit has a name and will respond to that name when met head-on by righteous prayer.

WARNING: Do not take this list lightly and go around using these names flippantly and carelessly. If you do, you will bring unnecessary harm to yourself. You should only use these names, as well as the name *Satan*, when you are combating spirits in warfare.

The devil is called…

Abaddon and Apollyon (which literally means destroyer)

And they had as king over them the angel of the bottomless pit, whose name in Hebrew is Abaddon, but in Greek he has the name Apollyon (Revelation 9:11).

Accuser of our brethren

Then I heard a loud voice saying in heaven, "Now salvation, and strength, and the kingdom of our God, and the power of His Christ have come, for the accuser of our brethren, who accused them before our God day and night, has been cast down" (Revelation 12:10).

Adversary

Be sober, be vigilant; because your adversary the devil walks about like a roaring lion, seeking whom he may devour (1 Peter 5:8).

Beelzebub

But some of them said, "He casts out demons by Beelzebub, the ruler of the demons" (Luke 11:15).

Belial

And what accord has Christ with Belial? Or what part has a believer with an unbeliever? (2 Corinthians 6:15)

Devil

Then Jesus, being filled with the Holy Spirit, returned from the Jordan and was led by the Spirit into the wilderness, being tempted for forty days by the devil. And in those days He ate nothing, and afterward, when they had ended, He was hungry (Luke 4:1-2).

Dragon

He laid hold of the dragon, that serpent of old, who is the Devil and Satan, and bound him for a thousand years; and he cast him into the bottomless pit, and shut him up, and set a seal on him, so that he should deceive the nations no more till the thousand years were finished. But after these things he must be released for a little while (Revelation 20:2-3).

Evil spirit

But the Spirit of the LORD departed from Saul, and an evil spirit from the LORD troubled him (1 Samuel 16:14, KJV).

Father of all lies

You are of your father the devil, and the desires of your father you want to do. He was a murderer from the beginning, and does not stand in the truth, because there is no truth in him. When he speaks a lie, he speaks from his own resources, for he is a liar and the father of it (John 8:44).

god of this age

But even if our gospel is veiled, it is veiled to those who are perishing, whose minds the god of this age has blinded, who do not believe, lest the light of the gospel of the glory of Christ, who is the image of God, should shine on them (2 Corinthians 4:3-4).

Great red dragon

And another sign appeared in heaven: behold, a great, fiery red dragon having seven heads and ten horns, and seven diadems on his heads (Revelation 12:3).

Lying spirit

The LORD said to him, "In what way?" So he said, "I will go out and be a lying spirit in the mouth of all his prophets." And the LORD said, "You shall persuade him, and also prevail. Go out and do so" (1 Kings 22:22).

Murderer

You are of your father the devil, and the desires of your father you want to do. He was a murderer from the beginning, and does not stand in the truth, because there is no truth in him.

When he speaks a lie, he speaks from his own resources, for he is a liar and the father of it (John 8:44).

Power of darkness

He has delivered us from the power of darkness and conveyed us into the kingdom of the Son of His love, in whom we have redemption through His blood, the forgiveness of sins (Colossians 1:13-14).

The prince/ruler of this world

Now is the judgment of this world; now the ruler of this world will be cast out. And I, if I am lifted up from the earth, will draw all peoples to Myself (John 12:31-32).

The prince of the power of the air

And you He made alive, who were dead in trespasses and sins, in which you once walked according to the course of this world, according to the prince of the power of the air, the spirit who now works in the sons of disobedience, among whom also we all once conducted ourselves in the lusts of our flesh, fulfilling the desires of the flesh and of the mind, and were by nature children of wrath, just as the others (Ephesians 2:1-3).

Ruler of the darkness of this age

For we do not wrestle against flesh and blood, but against principalities, against powers, against the rulers of the darkness of this age, against spiritual hosts of wickedness in the heavenly places (Ephesians 6:12).

Satan

And the God of peace will crush Satan under your feet shortly. The grace of our Lord Jesus Christ be with you. Amen (Romans 16:20).

Serpent

Then the serpent said to the woman, "You will not surely die" (Genesis 3:4).

Tempter

For this reason, when I could no longer endure it, I sent to know your faith, lest by some means the tempter had tempted you, and our labor might be in vain (1 Thessalonians 3:5).

Unclean spirit

When an unclean spirit goes out of a man, he goes through dry places, seeking rest, and finds none (Matthew 12:43).

Wicked one

When anyone hears the word of the kingdom, and does not understand it, then the wicked one comes and snatches away what was sown in his heart. This is he who received seed by the wayside (Matthew 13:19).

CHAPTER FOUR

THE WARFARE TACTICS OF KING DAVID

David is perhaps one of the most beloved characters in the entire Bible, next to Jesus. He is known as a shepherd, a writer, a poet, a psalmist, a musician, a lover, a kingly ruler, a prophet, a faithful confidant, a father, a husband, and a friend of God. Although David clearly shone in each of those capacities, David as a warrior tends to come through the pages of the Scriptures just as clearly as all the others combined. In his role as a warrior there are many lessons given to us that will help us become spiritual warriors as skilled as he was.

David fought many battles. He lived his life from childhood knowing in his heart that he was more spiritually proficient than some of the most experienced warriors of his day, even those who were far older and far more mature than he was. One of the major secrets that David grew up knowing was that he had a covenant with God. He was a circumcised Hebrew boy, which meant that God was obligated to protect his interests no matter how deadly his situation became. Knowing that information caused David to have a winning attitude at all times.

He knew that none of the battles he faced would be fought using only the power of his personal physical strength; rather, he would access the almighty power of God. That one distinction is the key to victorious warfare every single time. Know that God is fighting for you and that He is fighting through you. When you begin to see your own self as your source of power and strength, you will fail. It does not take much thought to recognize that both you and I have limited strength, skills, and resources at our disposal. God, on the contrary, has unlimited power and might and more strategies than one could ever dream of or even need.

You and I as believers have the same covenant that David had. Wait a minute—I think I should change that. No, you have an even *greater* covenant than David did because of Jesus' sacrificial death. And since we have a better promise, incorporated into that same equation are superior victories.

A key secret to spiritual warfare is knowing you have a covenant with God.

Many people whom I deal with and train to become spiritual warriors are eager to get to the hands-on, nitty gritty, practical approach to defeating devils. They want to know exactly what to do and how to do it. The real truth is that we need not try to do anything until we first know. The "knowing" precedes all practice. I've seen churches fail miserably within a few short months after opening up. I've witnessed itinerant ministers start off strong, traveling all around the country, only to suddenly realize that they are no longer a "hot commodity" and no one is inviting them to their churches anymore. Then they find themselves having to work a nine-to-five job again just to make ends meet.

Had they known that their calling was from God to begin with, they would never have had to change their careers so abruptly. When you know what God has called you to do and where God desires you to be, nothing in the world can change that. You know in your heart that if it's not working today, then it will work tomorrow. If I can't have what I need here, then I know that God will provide for me over there.

If it appears that the enemy has defeated me, it's only a setup against the devil to overthrow his entire agenda without his realizing it. It is a surprise attack offensive mechanism. When you know, you just know. And it is that knowledge of Whose you are and who you are in direct juxtaposition to God the Father that is the key element in winning the battles of your life.

KNOWING THE COVENANT-KEEPING GOD

For on the one hand there is an annulling of the former commandment because of its weakness and unprofitableness, for the law made nothing perfect; on the other hand, there is the bringing in of a better hope, through which we draw near to God. And inasmuch as He was not made priest without an oath (for they have become priests without an oath, but He with an oath by Him who said to Him: "The LORD has sworn and will not relent, 'You are a priest forever according to the order of Melchizedek' "), by so much more Jesus has become a surety of a better covenant (Hebrews 7:18-22).

According to the Book of Hebrews, Jesus has become the collateral for you and me to enjoy the benefits of a better covenant. When we are born into the body of the Lord Jesus Christ, we become circumcised through the shedding of His blood. When that happens, we, like God, become invincible in battle. Most students of the Holy Writ know well that David was not a born fighter. He did have somewhat of an intuitive knack for combat, though. For the most part, David was simply a shepherd boy with a passionate love for music. Shepherding is what David knew how to do well.

Music, too, was a very natural part of his biological makeup. In various accounts in the Scriptures we see David singing before the Lord. You can see accounts of this in Second Samuel 22 and in Psalms 7 and 18. He was made to sing. But since he was not made to fight, he had to use another approach to warring than the common methods employed by soldiers during his time. Why am I dealing with this topic in such an exhaustive manner? I have a feeling that you may not be a natural fighter.

If you are not, you may automatically exclude yourself from the battle because you don't have proclivities toward this kind of engagement. The battles will not be won as much with strategic tactics as by the intangibles. These are things like knowledge, perseverance, faith, dedication, love, forgiveness, and determination. These are the things that give you a capacity for allowing God to perform great and mighty miracles through you. Without these things, you stop up the flow of God's mighty hand working in your life. David walked in such a realization.

KILLING A LION AND A BEAR

A characteristic of true warriors is that they never allow their opponents to live; they always kill them. They don't kill them because they are cold and heartless. Rather, they do it out of protocol, out of obligation. If they don't kill the enemy, the enemy will rise up against them and kill them given the first opportunity. It's the same thing with sin and licentiousness. When it comes against you, you cannot merely cripple it and temporarily paralyze it; you have to kill it. If you don't believe me when I tell you that it will kill you, you had better reconsider you mindset. Kill the enemy!

So you have to become more aggressive when it comes to dealing with anything that can potentially destroy you. But how do you kill a lion and a bear? Do you know anyone personally who goes around killing jungle kings such as lions and mountain animals such as wild bears? I don't know anyone who has ever killed a lion or a bear. Maybe a squirrel or a raccoon came face to face with death while trying to cross my driving path, but that was only an accident.

You would have to be a highly skilled hunter to successfully kill these animals without incurring any sufficient wounds or coming near to death. We can again gather a tremendous amount of knowledge and insight from David as we observe his spiritual techniques in dealing with imminent death. There isn't one place in the text where you will find David attending classes on how to kill a bear and a lion.

No, he was not academically trained. The major point here is that some things you will never learn through applied learning. They simply have to be *caught* in the spirit realm. And the only way to catch the concept being taught is through engagement. I'm often amazed at how many young people complete four years of college yet, when they graduate, cannot find a job measuring up to the college training they received.

Time after time, I've seen young men and women fresh out of college be rejected because they lack work experience. Some things you will never learn until you just do it. That is one of the reasons it is so important for medical doctors to complete internships (on-the-job preliminary training) before they actually become full-fledged physicians. In fact, I personally believe that most jobs should require some level of on-the-job training before allowing people entry.

Some things you simply have to "catch."

This prerequisite should be especially mandated in the ministry where far too many people become pastors and church leaders, yet have never submitted or followed anyone closely since they received Christ. That's a whole book by itself! For now, realize that David caught spiritual directives while engaging in battle. He did not always know what to do and when to do it. But because he was obedient to the voice of the Lord, he knew God would lead him into victory, whether or not he had a blueprint to follow beforehand.

But David said to Saul, "Your servant used to keep his father's sheep, and when a lion or a bear came and took a lamb out of the flock, I went out after it and struck it, and delivered the lamb from its mouth; and when it arose against me, I caught it by its beard, and struck and killed it. Your servant has killed both lion and bear; and this uncircumcised Philistine will be like one of them, seeing he has defied the armies of the living God." Moreover David said, "The LORD, who delivered me from the paw of the lion and from the paw of the bear, He will deliver me from the hand of this Philistine." And Saul said to David, "Go, and the LORD be with you!" (1 Samuel 17:34-37)

Let's not look at this bear as simply a bear. As with any spiritual war, we must view this bear, although clearly an animal on the outside, as a spirit. And the spirit operating within this bear had an assignment from Satan to kill David and the innocent lamb. When you read the text, it clearly shows us that David was empowered to strike and kill the lion and the bear when he sensed that they could cause fatal harm to the lambs he was to care for. This act, among others, validated David's call to shepherding the sheep.

It also serves as a stellar example for pastors and local church leaders of how we should care for the sheep whenever wolf-like spirits come into our churches to prey on the parishioners. No matter in whom the evil spirit shows up, it is our responsibility to strike it down. Understand that onlookers may not immediately understand your motive. At first glance, you may appear to be the evil one and not the predator. But that's all right.

It really does not matter how onlookers perceive you when you are engaged in warfare. You must know that God's command to protect the sheep at any cost is far more important than a soulish misunderstanding. You have to move beyond that. Spiritual warriors cannot allow their feelings and emotions to hinder their progress. It is not that we are calloused people. No, it's not that at all. We have a job to do. The only way it will ever get done, however, is when we remain completely and totally focused. There is nothing as powerfully distracting as emotions and personal feelings. So you've got to beware of those kinds of things.

My final observation about this narrative is how quickly the focus shifts as a reminder not only to David but also to the reader of God's Word that God is the ultimate Deliverer, not us. If we could deliver ourselves, then we would not have need of a God.

In the first mention of the lion and the bear fight, David admitted to striking the beasts. But before the story was over, David gave the credit to whom it is always due: God. *"Moreover David said, 'The LORD, who delivered me from the paw of the lion and from the paw of the bear, He will deliver me from the hand of this Philistine.' "* Knowing that God delivered you before brings a tremendous encouragement and hope to know that He will do it again and again. Beforehand, before you engage in warfare, not only should you know that you are going to win; you should also know that God has already won the victory. That is how to kill a lion and a bear.

KILLING GOLIATH

So it was, when the Philistine arose and came and drew near to meet David, that David hurried and ran toward the army to meet the Philistine. Then David put his hand in his bag and took out a stone; and he slung it and struck the Philistine in his forehead, so that the stone sank into his forehead, and he fell on his face to the earth. So David prevailed over the Philistine with a sling and a stone, and struck the Philistine and killed him. But there was no sword in the hand of David. Therefore David ran and stood over the Philistine, took his sword and drew it out of its sheath and killed him, and cut off his head with it. And when the Philistines saw that their champion was dead, they fled (1 Samuel 17:48-51).

It is somewhat gruesome to think that someone could actually take another person's life. It is God who gives life, and He should be the only one to take it away, not man. So this story is not a justification of killing an individual who opposes you. In fact, this Scripture is not really trying to convey the sense of a human named Goliath being slaughtered at all. This act of destruction is directly opposing a spirit, one that is contrary to God. Realize that our enemy is very rarely a breathing person, a human with flesh and blood.

> *For we do not wrestle against flesh and blood, but against principalities, against powers, against the rulers of the darkness of this age, against spiritual hosts of wickedness in the heavenly places* (Ephesians 6:12).

The enemy is typically the contrary spirit that lives within others and lived within ourselves before we were born again. That is why the Scriptures command unbelievers to repent and be born again. *"Do not marvel that I said to you, 'You must be born again'"* (John 3:7). Until you are born again, you will consistently lose battles to the enemy within you. Many of the battles that you engage in take place on the battleground of your own mind. And far too often you can give too much credit to the enemy when you are under attack.

Regardless of how large you think your troubles are or how overwhelming the struggle has become, you will never win until you follow the example of David and begin to minimize the opposition. David never really saw Goliath as a giant. I realize that we've always been taught that David killed Goliath the giant. But in all fairness David the shepherd boy could not have killed a giant until he first saw himself as a bigger giant than the one he was facing.

Giants in life and in the spirit realm are all restricted. You are the one who gives any giant the ability to lord it over you. In fact, the extent to which you or I allow a giant to conquer us is the same degree to which we tread on the fringes of idolatry. Just to think that anything could actually be greater than the God within you places that thing above God. It really doesn't matter what the situation is or how troubling it is. Trouble will not last forever. What you believe to be a giant today will actually appear to be a dwarf years from now.

David was not physically stronger than the giant. He was not a more skilled fighter than Goliath. He knew nothing about guerrilla warfare tactics. Goliath, on the other hand, was a very skilled assassin. Not only did people fear him by reputation, but also the very sight of him petrified entire nations. Imagine that! One man had the power to instill fear in the

Begin to minimize the opposition

minds and spirits of nations. I am not sure what you think about this, but I believe that is too much power to give to anybody. For too long now, we have allowed the enemy's threats and manipulative tactics to intimidate us so badly that we have become incapacitated.

That has never been God's will. Honor man and fear God. That's how God established it. As soon as you begin to fear man, it immediately dishonors God. David, who seemingly should have had fear of the giant, particularly since his fellow brothers and the host of Israelites dreaded Goliath's presence, was not afraid. It is rather obvious that he understood the dynamics of Goliath's natural strength and might. He had also heard stories of how Goliath killed off scores of people at one time. Still David was unfazed.

The one thing David realized is that he had leverage. He had influence, not with man, but rather with God. He knew that he had a covenant with God while Goliath did not. Just knowing that fact alone caused him to rise up with such monumental faith that he knew he had won the fight long before he actually engaged in battle. From the very start to the end, David knew that he really did not have to fight at all.

He knew that God was fighting for him. That's one of the powerful secrets of spiritual warfare. You must know that the fight you are engaged in is really not your fight at all, but rather the Lord's. Defeat your giants not by using your strength, but the strength of the Lord. You will be victorious every time regardless of how enormous your giant may appear to be.

> *You are of God, little children, and have overcome them, because He who is in you is greater than he who is in the world* (1 John 4:4).

KNOWING WHEN TO HOLD 'EM AND FOLD 'EM

> *Then the men of David said to him, "This is the day of which the LORD said to you, 'Behold, I will deliver your enemy into your hand, that you may do to him as it seems good to you.' " And David arose and secretly cut off a corner of Saul's robe. Now it happened afterward that David's heart troubled him because he had cut Saul's robe. And he said to his men, "The LORD forbid that I should do this thing to my master, the LORD's anointed, to stretch out my hand against him, seeing he is the anointed of the LORD." So David restrained his servants with these words, and did not allow them to rise against Saul. And Saul got up from the cave and went on his way* (1 Samuel 24:4-7).

One of the warfare tactics or secrets of King David is that he knew that in order to have complete victory over the powers of hell, he would have to respect God's set protocol. Protocol is simply etiquette; from a godly perspective it is His way of doing things. When you operate within His system of protocol, you will always win and be victorious. Conversely, when you choose not to follow His protocol, you will inevitably and miserably fail.

King David knew the dangers of taking matters into his own hands. David knew that it was not by might nor by human power that his kingdom would be established. It would be established by the working of the Spirit of God. King David knew when to kill and when to stay his hand and let God have His way. Even though his mighty men rebuked him harshly when he refused to kill King Saul when he had him in his hands, David still did not find that a suitable reason to break rank with God's order.

King David was a man after God's own heart, and he fully realized that if he used his spiritual weaponry to kill God's anointed he would have released a curse against his own life. This respecting of God's order is a very interesting concept that we seem to have lost in the church. Far too many Christians falsely believe that when a God-appointed authority gets out of place, they have the right to deal with that person, correct that person, or even slander that person. I have witnessed how some Christian magazines slander people in the name of God. Their justification is that they are publishing the truth.

Respecting God's protocol is a key to victorious spiritual warfare.

Perhaps they are revealing the truth; however, all truth does not need to be revealed. Furthermore, there is a time and a season in which some truths actually need to be presented. In the same manner that you would try your best to shelter a child from illicit and vulgar influences, mature believers need to protect baby believers from being disturbed by things they are not spiritually equipped to handle.

The same Christian journals that tend to fight against fallen leaders rather than pray for them very seldom report on the truth concerning situations such as the hundreds of thousands of people being murdered in Darfur, Africa, and how our nation is doing little or nothing to help the situation. Truth is truth; if your objective is to deal forthrightly with the message of truth, let's be fair and not leave anything out.

You have to know what fight is actually your fight and which fight really belongs to the Lord. You will never win the fight that He is supposed to be fighting for you. He is able to win that fight, not you. Whether you like it or not, there are some areas that the common Christian simply does not have a right to deal with. It's beyond his scope of reasoning and authority.

Now, that does not give a person in authority, such as King Saul, the right to be abusive and manipulatively controlling. And I am not saying that you should stay in such an environment or remain in submission under a leader if you have been subjected to that kind of abuse. No, you should not stay in a place where someone is intentionally berating you and trying to kill you. Rather, you should remove yourself from unnecessary abuse and get planted somewhere you truly believe you will grow and prosper in the things of the Lord. It's not your job to fight leadership. I am totally convinced that God does a superb job when dealing with corrupted leadership. Again, it's His fight, not yours. David knew that God was a big enough God to fulfill His Word to him, without David having to avenge Saul on his own.

> *Dearly beloved, avenge not yourselves, but rather give place unto wrath: for it is written, Vengeance is mine; I will repay, saith the Lord* (Romans 12:19, KJV).

True spiritual warriors need to learn this important lesson from the life of King David. Vengeance belongs to the Lord. David knew that King Saul had an appointment with death. He also knew that he did not have to speed up God's process, as we so often try to do. One of the main reasons God does not use many believers as mightily as He would like to is that they do not know how to wait on God and attack only when God commands them to attack.

David's strategies of war kept changing from one battle to the next because each time he went to war, the Lord gave him a new strategy that took all his enemies by surprise. It was quite difficult for the enemies of King David to know what approach he was going to use every time they fought against him, since the old methods had been so quickly discarded.

With new and unorthodox military approaches coming straight from God, David confused his enemy over and over again. How do you fight your enemies? Do whatever God tells you to do. It's really that simple. But be careful to obey God when He tells you to do nothing. Sometimes doing nothing is the greatest thing you can actually do, and your obedience opens the door to God's miraculous power in your life.

> *Be still, and know that I am God; I will be exalted among the nations, I will be exalted in the earth!* (Psalm 46:10)

CHAPTER FIVE

DEAD MEN FIGHTING: WARRING AGAINST THE FLESH

I affirm, by the boasting in you which I have in Christ Jesus our Lord, I die daily (1 Corinthians 15:31).

W as the apostle Paul speaking morbidly when he said that he died daily? Not at all. Instead, Paul was talking of the secret to having life in the spirit. In order to experience life in the spirit and to be victorious in spiritual warfare, it is important to die daily to the desires of the flesh. The soul and the spirit are one and are never separated, unless it concerns a judicial matter in Scripture. Aside from that scenario, they are always one. But the spirit and the soul are both always at war with the flesh, and vice versa.

Why? The reason is simply that the flesh always does things and desires things that are directly opposing the spirit, or God's character. And when your flesh opposes the very nature of God, it limits your potency when dealing with adversarial spirits. Knowing that, Paul took the stance that he could not give his flesh any access to life, realizing that the smallest amount of access could cause his warfare to be hindered and his entire being to be vulnerable to the devil's attack.

He willfully chose the road less traveled, knowing that road was the divine pathway to a life of spiritual power and authority in God. Many of God's people become frightened when they think about this concept of dying daily, realizing that they have to cut away from some of the things they've held so dear. The mature in faith, though, know that without dying daily the release of genuine spiritual power is not possible.

DEAD MEN DON'T HAVE FEELINGS

I suspect that at some point in your life, you have been to a funeral of a friend or a loved one. So it's probably safe to assume that you have seen a dead body. During the final viewing, friends and family circle around the casket to catch a final glimpse of their loved one. When they look at the lifeless body of their departed friend or family member, they usually are taken aback by the complete lack of feeling and lifelessness of the departed.

Just for the sake of illustration, suppose some maniac began hurling insulting slurs at the person lying in the casket during the viewing. The person lying in state would not give any emotional response at all. In fact, the dead man or woman would not really care about what was being said. The onlookers and people bidding him or her farewell would be very insulted by the rudeness and insensitivity and would probably want to fight. What is the difference? The difference is that dead people cannot get hurt or offended by anything. That's the advantage that they have over the living. Nothing bothers them at all.

Nothing bothers the dead.

Imagine fighting an enemy who never gets angry, emotional, or fearful because they lack the ability to respond to feeling. It would actually cause you to be more cautious, since most people are apt to respond to every single offensive gesture. Getting offended tends to be the norm, so you would probably be seriously baffled by an enemy's capacity to not become offended. In fact, when people become offended, their offense opens the door to their own vulnerability.

This example has a very serious spiritual application. God can only use the spiritual warriors who have completely died to their own feelings and their own agendas. He uses those whose sole concern in life is to live for the glory of God. This kind of person does not vacillate between two opinions; such warriors are stable, much like Mount Zion, and cannot be moved or swayed by changing times. They choose never to get offended. As a result, these men and women continue to win the battle over their flesh, allowing their spirit to rule and reign as Christ so desires.

ONLY DEAD MEN CAN SEE GOD'S FACE

And he said, I beseech thee, show me thy glory....And he said, Thou canst not see my face: for there shall no man see me, and live (Exodus 33:18,20, KJV).

Only the dead can see God. Since God is Spirit, He cannot be revealed to anything other than spirit. So in order to see Him, your flesh has to die. Your fleshly desires and humanistic inner longings have to die. No man can see God and live. One of the most powerfully anointed characters in the Bible would have to be the man Moses. Moses was given a greater dimension of spiritual authority than any other of God's prophets in the Old Testament. Moses single-handedly brought the great nation of Egypt to its knees through the power of an almighty God.

When he lifted up his rod, signs, miracles, and wonders took place. When he lifted his rod, the Red Sea immediately opened up and God's people safely passed through the sea on dry land. Although he had seen the miraculous as few have before his time or even after, Moses still knew that there was so much more to God than he had experienced. Moses hungered for God to the point that nothing in life satisfied him more than to spend even one moment with Him. Spiritual hunger for more of God began to rise within Moses' spirit until it became a relentless hurricane of holy desire.

Finally he mustered up the courage to beseech God, *"Show me Your glory!"* To which the Lord responded, *"Moses, no one can see My face and live!"* When I heard this Scripture taught early in my Christian walk, most preachers taught it from the angle that no one could look at God and expect to live. In other words, they'd die right on the spot. That is not exactly what this Scripture is saying.

What it is conveying is the concept that anything that is not like God has to die in His presence. It cannot live. God is a holy God, so He requires holiness. And no matter which way you present it, flesh is not and cannot be holy. All flesh is corrupt. So the only way you can present yourself to God is to die to the flesh so that your spirit will live. You have to willfully become a living sacrifice.

> *I beseech you therefore, brethren, by the mercies of God, that you present your bodies a living sacrifice, holy, acceptable to God, which is your reasonable service* (Romans 12:1).

Dead men are men who have forfeited their passion and desire to pursue their own fleshly agenda. They caught a glimpse of the glory of God and were instantly transformed for the rest of their lives. They live for nothing other than experiencing more of God. They are worshipping warriors. What the world has to offer these folks has lost its appeal.

These people are not dead because of the absence of physical life; rather, they have no will of their own. They have fought their way into a place where their will has become meshed with the will of God. These are the true spiritual warriors of the kingdom of God. God can trust them with great spiritual authority and power. And because they have no personal agenda, they'll get His job done.

THE GREATEST FIGHT IS WITH YOU

But I keep under my body, and bring it into subjection: lest that by any means, when I have preached to others, I myself should be a castaway (1 Corinthians 9:27, KJV).

The body of Christ is full of believers who don't mind chasing devils all over town. They love to cast devils out of other people, but they have never fought with the devil within. To them spiritual warfare is all about doing warfare with principalities and powers in the heavenly realms and casting demons out of other people here on earth. Even though what they are doing is a part of the total package, they are unfortunately missing a major portion of what spiritual warfare is all about. The greatest fight you will ever have is the one against your own fleshly nature.

If the truth were told, much of the pain that many churchgoers deal with from day to day was not scheduled by Satan but by their own foolish and selfish choices. The things that they attribute to the works of Satan have very little to do with Satan and a lot with their own fleshly nature. Because I deal in this area of spiritual warfare in my ministry, I have come to accept the truth that no one is really ready to be released into spiritual warfare on behalf of another person until he or she has first conquered the battle in his or her own flesh.

Your greatest fight is against your own flesh.

That is your proving ground to deal with greater fights. Satan will literally kill anyone who approaches him who is not qualified to confront his power. Just because you say, "In the name of Jesus" does not mean that Satan is going to run away from you. In fact, he might use the name of Jesus right back at you. What Satan recognizes and is most afraid of is the believer who knows the authority that he or she has in Christ. And that authority comes only after you have proved its power working in your own life.

One of the apostle Paul's greatest fears was the possibility of being disqualified from entering God's heavenly kingdom by living a lifestyle totally out of control. Paul knew that it was very much possible to be a great preacher, winning thousands of souls to the kingdom of God, and still be cast away from God's presence as profane. This is not to say that God expects you and me to live a lifestyle of perfection by man's standards. Both you and I know that God is a loving and forgiving God.

However, there are some things that enter into the flesh when we give it an allowance that are extremely difficult to eliminate once they are there. It's not that God cannot cleanse you from all unrighteousness; He can. But the chances that you will submit yourself to His cleansing process may be pretty unlikely, particularly if you have come to enjoy your fleshly choices.

One sin leads to another, which leads to another. After a while, you'll be amazed by how corrupted your inner man has become. Much like cancer in its early stages can be treated, so can the works of your flesh. But if you wait to deal with it in its final stages, it may be too late. Deal with your own self early on, so that God won't have to later.

JUDAS—A GREAT SPIRITUAL WARRIOR

After Judas Iscariot's historical betrayal, he was filled with an overwhelming sense of depression and personal remorse when he realized the result of his actions. When he saw the sufferings that Jesus endured because of his act of betrayal, he suddenly lost the appetite for the 30 pieces of silver that the Pharisees had given him in exchange for betraying his Lord. Judas Iscariot ended up committing suicide. What a tragedy!

Why did this happen? This could all have been avoided. Sadly, Judas Iscariot, like so many of God's people, did not realize that his greatest fight was not with demons and devils, but with his own nature. I am convinced that God had a promising destiny for Judas Iscariot. He was originally chosen to be one of the 12 founding apostles. He also was called to be an eyewitness to Jesus' majestic glory and to the power of the kingdom of God. There was a spiritual warrior trapped within his fleshly nature longing to get out.

The interesting thing here is this: Many people whose actions are quite contrary to their calling in life are fighting a battle within. The spiritual warrior is trying to come out of them, yet they are subconsciously continuing to allow their old spiritual nature to surface. We know that Judas had a knack for handling finances and that he functioned in some capacity of business prior to his conversion. It is quite possible that Judas was a notorious thief; his later actions surely proved that he had those tendencies. When he began to follow Jesus, though, there are just some things about his nature that refused to die.

When you are born again, there are some things that you should expect God to sanctify about your character and embellish for the glory of His kingdom. For example, if a person is really aggressive and demanding in his or her unsaved state, after that person has received salvation, he or she should not lose that aggressiveness but should rather begin using it for God's glory and His kingdom.

Don't throw away aggressiveness, garrulousness, inner drive, or strong compassion. Instead, shift the focus of those qualities to work on behalf of Christ and His kingdom. Doing that will crucify the negative connections that your flesh formerly associated with those qualities. Quite unfortunately, Judas went to hell after he committed suicide. Imagine, someone clearly called to be a warrior for Christ winds up in the infernos of hell because he betrayed God.

I know that for most believers the thought of betraying God probably seems pretty impossible. But before you discard that thought, just think about Judas Iscariot. He was called to be a warrior but died in a war. Who were his opponents? Was it the devil? Was it perhaps the Pharisees? Maybe he was framed for a crime that he did not commit. None of those things are true. He died in a war against his own self. In the war against your own self, I sincerely pray and believe that you will come out a winner.

LYING TO GOD

But Peter said, Ananias, why hath Satan filled thine heart to lie to the Holy Ghost, and to keep back part of the price of the land? (Acts 5:3, KJV).

Two of the more tragic deaths of the post-Pentecost, apostolic era were the untimely deaths of a couple by the name of Ananias and Sapphira. They were members of the church at Jerusalem, and one day they decided to sell a piece of property and completely pledged all the proceeds to go to the Lord's house. When they finally sold the piece of property, they couldn't see themselves giving the full amount of their vow. Instead of going to the apostles and telling them that they were having second thoughts about their original pledge, they decided to act as if they were giving their full pledge.

Believing that they could defraud God and His people, they brought a partial offering to church. When they took their offering to the apostles, the Holy Spirit revealed to the apostle Peter that they were lying. The apostle Peter rebuked them for agreeing to try to deceive the Holy Spirit. When the apostle Peter exposed their devious lie through the word of knowledge, the power of the Holy Spirit struck both Ananias and his wife, and they died instantly.

It seemed to have happened so quickly. What in God's name had gone wrong? Just because they were a married couple does not mean that they had to agree on everything. I've seen husbands and wives leave churches where they both knew they were called to serve and grow. But because one became disgruntled, the other chose to follow instead of staying and doing what was right. All agreement is not good agreement, especially when it involves agreeing against God.

Ananias and Sapphira had opened a door to Satan through their flesh to attack the work of God and make a mockery of the Holy Spirit. Using the spirit of greed that was deeply imbedded in their old fleshly nature, Satan was able to fill their hearts with ravenous deception. If only they had realized that their greatest warfare was with their own fleshly nature, they would have saved themselves from this tragic end. Spiritual warfare is really serious business. And the war inside should be the first one fought. Don't think for a moment that you or anyone else can conspire against God and win.

Spiritual warfare is really serious business.

WARRING AGAINST THE FLESH

What does it actually mean to war against your flesh? Let's explore this concept. First let's identify what the word *flesh* actually means in the Scriptures. For the most part in the Scriptures, there are two primary schools of thought concerning the concept of flesh.

The flesh is the physical body in which our spirit man lives.

The flesh is the fallen nature of mankind and the sin that we inherited through our spiritual connection with the first Adam.

THE FLESH AS THE PHYSICAL BODY

The Scriptures teach us that we are to love our bodies and take very good care of them. Unfortunately, many Christians lack good practical teaching concerning their bodies and treat them like enemies rather than friends. Some neglect common health sense and ignore spending any time on the outward man, falsely believing that it would be worldly to do so.

This is a gross mistake because the body is very spiritual to God. First, because your body has been redeemed by the precious death and blood of the Lord Jesus Christ, it should hold a very high value in your eyes. The Bible declares that your body is no longer yours, but belongs exclusively to God because He paid a lofty price for it. The body is not to be treated like garbage. When you do treat it badly, you insult what Jesus actually went through to pay the price for you. God has even promised to destroy those who destroy the body.

It is not that God is going around seeking out people to destroy; that's the devil's job. But God's warning is more of a self-protective mechanism built into humanity. Let's face it, you fully understand how this principle works when it comes to taking care of your car, your home, or even "dry clean only" clothes. If you don't put oil in your car's engine, it will eventually fail. Or if you put water instead of gasoline in your car tank, it will impair its ability. If you fail to paint your wood home, the wood will in time become rotten, demanding even greater attention. You should care so much more for the body that Christ gave you, keeping it well long enough to fulfill your life's assignment.

Secondly, the body has to be viewed a bit differently than mere flesh because it literally houses the Spirit. And because God's Spirit is so prized, we must make sure that it has a clean house to live in. If Jesus came to your house or apartment and planned to stay just one night, how would you prepare the house for His visit? I would imagine that you would go to great lengths to ensure that your Lord had the most comfortable stay and the most enjoyable experience ever.

Your house wouldn't be filthy and unkempt, but spotless, or at least as good as you could get it. Now think about the fact that God has His permanent address in you. He lives in you, not just overnight, but all the time. Knowing that, you should be very careful to keep your body in the most cleansed state possible, trying not to offend the Holy Spirit because of your discretionary living.

Flee sexual immorality. Every sin that a man does is outside the body, but he who commits sexual immorality sins against his own body. Or do you not know that your body is the temple of the Holy Spirit who is in you, whom you have from God, and you are not your own? For you were bought at a price; therefore glorify God in your body and in your spirit, which are God's

(1 Corinthians 6:18-20).

The Bible tells us that without the spirit the body is dead, and without the body the spirit of man cannot function on the earth. If you lose your body through ignorance and neglect, you will have to leave this planet whether you have finished your divine assignment or not. The body is a good thing and is extremely important to God and the call of God on your life. So when you talk of warring with the flesh, you are not talking about fighting against or despising your own body.

THE FLESH AS THE FALLEN NATURE OF MANKIND AND THE SIN WE INHERITED

When we talk about warring against the flesh, we are talking about actively and purposefully resisting yielding to the worldly desires of our fallen nature. The carnal nature is the inherent desire to sin that dwells in the souls of all men and women because of the fall of Adam and Eve in the Garden of Eden.

The carnal nature is that inner reckless and rebellious voice that continuously gives us suggestions that are diametrically opposed to the will of God for our lives. The carnal or flesh nature is that instinctive response that makes even little children hide or tell a lie when they know they have done something wrong. This is what the Bible seriously warns us against. The carnal nature is Satan's life reigning through our members. It we give in to that nature, it will eventually kill us.

WARRING IS WORSHIP

I beseech you therefore, brethren, by the mercies of God, that you present your bodies a living sacrifice, holy, acceptable unto God, which is your reasonable service (Romans 12:1).

In this passage of Scripture, the beloved apostle Paul was making a heartfelt plea to the saints at Rome to present their bodies as a living sacrifice unto God. He called this process our only reasonable service unto God. The phrase *reasonable service* means that presenting our body as a living sacrifice is the least we can do for the Lord in response to all that He has done for us. When we war against our fleshly nature so that we can present our bodies as a living sacrifice to God, we actually worship God in the manner in which He desires to be worshipped.

The reason you continue to war in the spirit is because you already know the outcome.

So many people become somewhat disheartened and tired when fighting for God. I hope that it encourages you to know that not only is your war a meaningful one, but it is also a war that translates into worship before the Lord. When God sees that you refuse to give up in life and that you will not quit, but rather keep fighting, He receives that as praising His name. He sees that as giving Him your confidence. The reason you continue to war in the spirit is because you already know the outcome.

You know that God has already fixed the fight so that you will win. And it brings great pleasure to God when He recognizes that you have that much faith in Him. The phrase, a living sacrifice, *also compares the vast difference between the Old Testament sacrifices and the New Testament Sacrifice that God was looking for. In the Old Testament the sacrifice laid on the altar was a "dead sacrifice," but in the New Testament God introduced the concept of a "living sacrifice." God no longer needs dead sacri-*

fices because the death of the Lord Jesus Christ accomplished that once and for all.

CHAPTER SIX

WARRING WITH GOD

Many people have come to understand what it means to experience a war within. But few if any have ever settled within themselves the idea of warring against a mighty God. Although a few may understand what it really means to war with God, many others have experienced this phenomenon without realizing it. Those who haven't been able to label their encounter will inevitably have to repeat it. One thing I do know is that if you have never encountered a battle with Deity, you will at some point in your lifetime. Guaranteed.

Every believer at one time or another will come face to face with God. At times this encounter will happen at the point of initial conversion. At other times it may occur when one is trying to escape his or her calling to do God's will, much like Jonah did. Everyone who has ever run from God knows all too well what this fight actually feels like. Quite interestingly, it may seem as if fighting with God is a useless experience, futile at best.

But warring with God has some unusual benefits that only come through this face-to-face battle. Something literally happens to you when you strive with the Lord. It's a bit difficult to put into words, but I'll do my best. You become transformed into His image when you hold on to Him, whether He shakes you or embraces you. If you are believing God for a higher calling, an elevation in the spirit, you will definitely go through this process. Be encouraged, though, knowing that there are many who have gone through and come out of the fire as gold, and so will you.

The refining pot is for silver and the furnace for gold, but the LORD tests the hearts (Proverbs 17:3).

Behold, I have refined you, but not as silver; I have tested you in the furnace of affliction (Isaiah 48:10).

JACOB: A BORN WARRIOR

Jacob had an amazing encounter with God. Long before this encounter ever occurred, though, the infrastructure for his brush with the Lord had already begun. The conception of Esau and his twin brother Jacob was a miracle that came immediately after Isaac prayed to God asking Him to break the spirit of barrenness on his wife Rebekah. During her pregnancy Rebekah experienced excruciating pains as the babies inside her womb *wrestled* against each other—a foreshadowing of what was to come. In her dejected state Rebekah went and inquired of the Lord; she wanted to know exactly what was happening inside her womb.

The Lord told her that she was carrying twin babies. These babies were no common babies, but ones who represented the birthing of two nations. The older of the twins would eventually serve the younger. When they were finally born, Esau came out first, but Jacob's hand held tightly to his heel. This act of war was Jacob's very first feat as he entered into the earth. When Rebekah looked at him she knew intuitively that she had given birth to a fighter, a spiritual warrior. She named him *Jacob*, which means "one who supplants or deceives."

It is very possible that Rebekah told Jacob the prophecy that

God had given her about him becoming far greater and more powerful than his elder brother Esau. As Jacob grew older, he set his sights on stripping his elder brother of the blessing of the firstborn, Esau's birthright. His fighting tactics were so deceitful, yet skillful, that he succeeded in deceiving his father Isaac and stealing the blessing that Isaac had intended to pass on to Esau. When Esau discovered that Jacob stole his birthright, he vowed to kill him. Fearful, Jacob went into exile in the land of Syria to flee his brother's wrath.

Although he was far from home, far from his brother, he still had to fight battles. If you are a true spiritual warrior, it may appear that your battles never end. But with each battle you become wiser, and you begin to know how to measure each fight. Some fights are not worth too much attention, while others are more significant. Even in the land of Syria Jacob had to battle with his deceiving uncle Laban, who was underhandedly and constantly changing his wages. Instead of fighting his uncle in a conventional sense, he learned how to wage war by simply waiting.

Although he wrestled with so many different situations, nothing in Jacob's past profile of spiritual battles would have prepared him for the greatest fight of his life—his fight with God. Now I realize that this statement may arouse anger in some people, particularly the religious people who may view that statement as being sacrilegious. In your mind you ask, "How can a mere human fight with God?"

Some may passionately scream, "Heresy!" Yet the Scriptures are filled with several powerful examples of men warring with God. Unfortunately, because so many people don't realize this, many well-meaning believers are not very successful at the art of spiritual warfare. This experience with God is the necessary training that everyone must go through to achieve victory not just once in a while, but all the time.

LORD, WILL YOU SPAR WITH ME?

I believe that natural examples can often help us to more clearly understand spiritual truths. To help us fully appreciate this powerful concept of releasing the warrior within through warring with God, let's take a quick tour through a boxing gym. When boxing trainers are training a world-class boxer for the heavyweight championship title, they can't afford to leave any stones unturned. They make sure that their boxer is exposed to a wide variety of physical exercises to ensure that his body is in the best shape possible.

The boxer is told to lift weights that toughen his muscles and increase his punching power. The trainer makes the fighter run marathons to increase his fighter's level of endurance. The trainer then subjects his boxer to a series of mental tests to help him develop the mental and psychological toughness he needs to win the upcoming fight. Winning the championship title is not solely a physical feat, but also requires a certain frame of mind.

God becomes our sparring Partner to train us for the big fight. After all that, the trainer subjects his championship boxer to his ultimate test. He places his boxer in a boxing ring to fight against another highly skilled sparring partner. The purpose of the sparring partner is to simulate the dynamics and feelings of the actual championship fight. The trainer instructs his boxer to visualize the real championship fight and see his sparring partner as his real championship contender.

As the championship boxer spars with his sparring partner, inherent weaknesses or flaws in the boxing skills of the champion boxer, weaknesses of which the boxer was not even aware, are quickly revealed and corrected by the trainer. The sparring partner is also encouraged to taunt or mock the boxer in training to provoke anger in him, making him fight more passionately. The champion boxer is subjected to several of these sparring matches until the trainer is

90

fully satisfied that the flaws of his trainee are no longer present and the fighter is ready for real combat with an actual opponent.

This training example helps to plainly illustrate the Bible's depiction of what warring with God is all about. God puts us in a fighting ring with Himself and then suddenly begins throwing punches in our direction to see how well we can use the spiritual weapons He has given us to fight an actual spiritual enemy.

Warring with God in no way implies that we are in the same class as God. God is God all by Himself. He is in a class all by Himself. What it does imply is that God likes to become our sparring Partner as He teaches our hands to do war and our fingers to fight. This is what King David meant when he declared, *"Blessed be the LORD my Rock, who trains my hands for war, and my fingers for battle"* (Psalm 144:1).

I WON'T BACK UP NO MORE

After 20 years of living in exile, away from the land of his birth and promise, Jacob got homesick and desired to return to the land of his nativity. Jacob gathered his family and all his possessions and headed toward the land in which he was born. When he got close to the land, the news began to spread: Jacob was returning home. His old nemesis and brother Esau got wind that he had moved back. Esau had never resolved his issue with Jacob and had not forgiven his brother's devious deed in stealing his birthright and deceiving their ailing father.

When Esau heard the news of his brother's return, he quickly rallied 400 men of war and headed in Jacob's direction. After Jacob realized that his brother was again in pursuit of him with the intention of killing him, he began to panic. Quite naturally one would think that after two decades you could return to your former land, even if the reason you left suddenly was because of being on bad terms with an enemy. The elapsed time should have helped to erase the negative things done in the past. After all, Jacob had been quite a bit younger when he had made the choice to defraud his brother. Now he was much older and perhaps far more responsible than he had been before.

Like all warriors, Jacob had to experience moments of fear. Faith is not the absence of fear, but rather the ability to confront danger head-on despite the fear. The past had come full circle and was now ready to repay him for his deeds. In the past Jacob could simply grab his belongings and run. Now he was not a single man anymore. This time would not be so easy. He was now the husband of two wives who had given him many sons and a daughter. Jacob was now a father and husband, so he had no choice but to face his brother—even if it was only for the sake of his posterity.

The confrontation was inevitable, and Jacob began to prepare himself for it. He realized that even if he wanted to, he could no longer back up. He had to fight forward.

Jacob realized that his only chance at survival was to find God, and find Him quickly. This man knew the only thing that could save him was the fulfillment of the prophecy God had spoken to his mother prior to his birth.

The testimony of this unfulfilled prophecy was that Jacob was going to become greater and more powerful than his elder brother Esau. Put in the context of this writing, Jacob realized that there was a warrior within that had not yet been released. Jacob understood that in order to release the spiritual warrior trapped within, he would have to get his directives from God. Neither his flesh nor his conniving ways could give him what he wanted or save him this time; only God could. Jacob came to understand that he was finally living in the moment to which God had been trying to bring him his entire life.

God loves it when His men and women of war are in a place

where they cannot back up any further. This is the place of total and complete dependence on Him. Believers typically wait until they've lost much or are in need of much before they realize the need to be totally dependent on the Lord. The fight of your life will never really start until your back is against the wall. God does not want you to have any backing other than Himself. It's the only place where true victory happens. For Jacob, being in this uncomfortable position had been God's plan all along.

ROSA PARKS—WAR IN A MOMENT'S TIME

Legendary civil rights activist Rosa Parks did more to prove her ability to fight in a short moment than many have done in a lifetime. She was asked by a white man to give up her seat on a bus. When asked to do this before, she had willingly succumbed to the demands since they were the commonly accepted laws in Alabama. But one day when asked the same question, her response was surprisingly different. Rosa Parks decided that she was never going to give up her seat to a white person again.

She reached the point where her back was against the wall. She defiantly and boldly stood up against a discriminatory system that she believed was dehumanizing her and other African-Americans solely on the basis of color. Her one silent act literally altered the course of an entire nation, awakening its moral conscience. Rosa Parks had released the warrior within because she got to the place were she was tired of backing up. It did not take long for her to make a statement and begin a revolution—only a moment.

Here's a point to commit to your heart. Every fight does not necessarily have to be a long one or a vocal one. Very often God will get glory and give you victory in your silence. It is not so much what you say or even what you do. The true warriors just manifest who they are and what they stand for whether they verbalize it or not. Who you are will emerge when it's inside you. The fight always begins and ends within you.

Let be and be still, and know (recognize and understand) that I am God. I will be exalted among the nations! I will be exalted in the earth! (Psalm 46:10, AMP)

ALONE WITH GOD

Then Jacob was left alone; and a Man wrestled with him until the breaking of day. Now when He saw that He did not prevail against him, He touched the socket of his hip; and the socket of Jacob's hip was out of joint as He wrestled with him. And He said, "Let Me go, for the day breaks." But he said, "I will not let You go unless You bless me!" So He said to him, "What is your name?" He said, "Jacob." And He said, "Your name shall no longer be called Jacob, but Israel; for you have struggled with God and with men, and have prevailed" (Genesis 32:24-28).

So Jacob called the name of the place Peniel: "For I have seen God face to face, and my life is preserved." Just as he crossed over Penuel the sun rose on him, and he limped on his hip. Therefore to this day the children of Israel do not eat the muscle that shrank, which is on the hip socket, because He touched the socket of Jacob's hip in the muscle that shrank (Genesis 32:30-32).

The Bible tells us that Jacob was left alone at a place called Peniel by the banks of the river Jabok. When he found himself alone, he had an angelic visitation. This angel was not the typical depiction of an angel, but rather looked like a man. And this man began wrestling with Jacob. Many theologians believe that the angel of the Lord that appeared to Jacob was a "pre-New Testament" physical manifestation of Christ. Notice, though, that God did not appear to Jacob until he was *"left alone."* This is one of the most powerful secrets to tapping into your spiritual power. Don't be afraid to be left alone with God.

Far too many Christians only connect with God during times of public worship. They do not know how to relate to God in an intimate way when they are all by themselves. This is tragic indeed because it traps and stifles the spirit. There are things God can do for you when the crowd is around, but the most powerful, intimate, and life-altering things that God does only happen when you are left alone with Him. This is what happened to Jacob. Personal solitude and consecration are both divine prerequisites for releasing God's power within you.

Throughout the Scriptures there are accounts of people who experienced the zeniths of their lives when they were alone. Moses was alone on the back side of the desert when God found him, changed him, and released the warrior lying dormant inside him. The prophet Isaiah was alone in the temple in the year that King Uzziah died. That same year he was transformed into a warrior for God. The prophet Ezekiel was alone by the river Chebar in the land of Babylon when God found him and made him a spiritual warrior.

Mary was alone when the angel Gabriel appeared to her from the throne of God and told her that she was going to give birth to the Messiah through the power of the Holy Spirit. It's only when you are left alone that God can deal with things in your life that you were too distracted or embarrassed to deal with when everyone else was around. Many Christians fear being left alone, with no one to speak to but God. They will quickly get on the phone just to talk to somebody rather simply wait on the Lord.

The reason they use the phone, the Internet, digital cable, or a movie as an escape is that most people are afraid of what they may discover about themselves while spending time alone with God. Most people realize that God already knows everything about them. It's we who are afraid of our own selves. We know that God will deal with the secret places in our life when we are alone. Some simply are not ready to face the changes that God will require of them after such an encounter. So they delay the process. However, you will

95

never be all that God planned for you to become until you willingly take the step and spend time with Him, all alone.

THE BREAKING OF A NEW DAY

When Jacob began to wrestle with the angel of the Lord, he stubbornly refused to let go until the angel agreed to bless him. It's interesting to note that the Bible tells us the angel "wrestled" with him instead of "boxed" with him. Wrestling is one of the most physically involving combats of all mortal encounters. It demands the use of every limb of your body in order to win. Boxing, on the other hand, only requires the use of your hands. In boxing you are only allowed to hit certain parts of the body. Not following the rules could actually get you disqualified from the match. In a wrestling competition, every muscle is involved and you can pretty much hit any part of your opponents' body.

Why would God choose a wrestling match when He cornered Jacob as opposed to boxing him? I believe it's because God wanted to test Jacob in every way possible to determine just how hungry and desperate he was for God's hand to move in his life. Jacob knew that a genuine experience with God, an authentic blessing, was not merely the acquisition of more stuff. He realized it would actually change his character, giving him faith for fear and instilling within him the ability to face every challenge in his life and win.

During Jacob's struggle with God, the angel of the Lord pleaded with Jacob to let him go, but Jacob would not hear of it. Jacob was too close to getting what he wanted from God; he was not ready or willing to let go. Jacob told the angel that he would not let him go until he blessed him! This cry for the angel of the Lord to bless him is worth investigating.

It was obvious from the number of his vast possessions that God had blessed him; so why would Jacob cry out for more blessings? What blessing was Jacob asking for? I believe it was the prophetic blessing that God had promised through the prophecy given to Jacob's mother concerning him. Jacob was telling the heavenly envoy that he was not going to let go until God had honored the promise that He had made to his mother. This is what it means to war with God.

Warring with Him means that you are contending with God concerning the promises that He has already made to you that have not yet come to pass. Warring with God involves us going to God in heartfelt humility and spiritual hunger and declaring that we will not be moved until He has fulfilled all that He promised us. The Bible also tells us that Jacob fought with the angel till the "*breaking of day.*" What does this statement mean?

It means that once we have cornered God in our spiritual pursuit, we are not to let go of our hold on Divinity until there is a complete change in our situation. We have to come into a new day. The warrior within must be released so he can take over. Unfortunately, most Christian believers do not know this type of unwavering posture in the place of prayer because we live in a spoiled microwave generation that is impatient and indifferent toward the concept of waiting on God.

This microwave generation wants things to happen quickly, within a short period of time, or they will move on to something else. This impatient attitude will not release the warrior within; neither will it move the hand of God on your life. When it comes to releasing the warrior within, God refuses to be rushed. God will not release great authority and power in the lives of those who are too much in a hurry to wait for Him to complete His process. The warrior within them will remain trapped in obscurity until they become willing and hungry enough to war with God for their destiny, even if it means waiting until the breaking of a new day.

WHAT IS YOUR NAME?

When the angel of the Lord was fully convinced that Jacob was serious with God and that he was not going to let go until he received the prophetic promise, the celestial messenger asked him a very interesting question. *"What is your name?"* Jacob must have been baffled by the question and wondered what the connection was between his name and the prophetic blessing that he was pursuing. *"My name is Jacob,"* he replied. The angel of the Lord quickly responded and said, *"Your name shall no longer be Jacob, but Israel; because as a prince you have prevailed with both God and man!"*

Suddenly Jacob felt an anointed surge rush through him that he had never felt before. He felt like a man who had been reborn. He felt a sense and an air of confidence. The fears that once plagued him dissipated like the evaporated morning dew during a sunny day. He felt as though he could conquer the world and defeat any demon Satan would send his way. Like a prisoner who had lived in solitary confinement for many years and was suddenly released to look into the sun, Jacob was free.

The moment his name changed, Jacob suddenly realized that "Jacob" was the name of the loser who had acquired everything through deceit and manipulation. Israel was the name of his spiritual warrior who had been trapped in his fleshly lifestyle, waiting to reveal the authentic. The people of the ancient world believed that a man could never live above the true meaning of his name. They believed that a man's name and his nature were intricately intertwined, like delicate strands of the same cloth.

The ancients believed that a man's spiritual identity and destiny were all wrapped up in his name. Take Jacob. His name meant "supplanter or one who deceives," and when you look at the earlier years of his life before this God encounter, his behavior certainly fit his name. God could not release the warrior within until He had changed Jacob's spiritual identity. This is what warring with God does for us. It releases us into our true spiritual identity and permanently erases our negative past.

YOUR STRUGGLE HAS TO END IN VICTORY

Before the angel of the Lord left, he dislocated Jacob's hip, but he also blessed him and released him into his prophetic promise. As Jacob walked away from his divinely ordained struggle, he was limping pretty severely, but his spirit had never felt livelier. There was a supernatural power for victory flowing through his spirit that he had never experienced before. He knew that the fear he had for Esau was now gone. In its place was an aura of dominion over the powers of hell.

Jacob received a name change. He went from Jacob the con artist to the mighty nation of Israel, which means "he who rules as God rules." When God changes your name, your character changes simultaneously. In fact, your name mirrors your character. It's no surprise at all that when Esau and his 400 men of war showed up, Jacob sought peace instead of war. His struggle with the angel had ended in his victory. His decisions from that moment on were no longer based totally upon the will of his flesh but rather on the will of God. Don't shun your struggle; it is the only door to your victory.

Without a struggle, there can be no progress.
—*Frederick Douglass*

CHAPTER SEVEN

HITTING THE TARGET

I therefore so run, not as uncertainly; so fight I, not as one that beateth the air (1 Corinthians 9:26, KJV).

CASUALTIES OF FRIENDLY FIRE

Imagine if you ran a 26.2-mile marathon and won the race, but afterward discovered that you were not scheduled to run that particular race. You would be most depressed. And you'd feel a sense of great regret over the wasted time and energy preparing for the wrong race. The apostle Paul intentionally lived his life so that every area of his life and everything he did was aimed in a very specific direction. There are too many Christians doing spiritual warfare who have no clue as to what they are really doing.

The apostle Paul described this practice as "beating the air." Have you ever stood in the middle of the road on a very windy day and tried to beat the wind with your fists? How much pain and suffering did you inflict on the wind from your swift and strong blows? It did not affect the wind at all. Hopefully you are beginning to see the wisdom in this illustration. It's a waste of time and energy to try to beat up the wind.

Ever since the United States government led an attack against

Iraq and Afghanistan, there have been hundreds of United States soldiers who have been killed by friendly fire. *Friendly fire* is a military term used to describe the killing or injury of soldiers by its own soldiers, who mistook them for enemy combatants. There is nothing more tragic than the killing of allies by allies because of human error or mistaken identity. The body of Christ is full of men and women who have been spiritually killed or seriously injured by other believers who mistook them for the enemy. This is tragic indeed.

This is why the apostle Paul admonished all believers to make sure they correctly identify their target of attack before they start shooting into the realms of the spirit. In the military when the same soldier is caught shooting at his fellow soldiers more than once—because he continues to mistake his fellow soldiers for the enemy—that soldier will be recalled and then court martialed.

Such soldiers will lose their rank and authority in the military. I really believe that's one of the reasons some believers who used to flow in the power of God no longer do so. They kept abusing their spiritual power and shooting at fellow Christians. God has since removed their authority and pulled their rank. God does want us to fight and overcome the powers of hell, but He wants us to know where the real target is and shoot only at it.

TARGET PRACTICE

> *For every one that useth milk is unskilful in the word of righteousness: for he is a babe. But strong meat belongeth to them that are of full age, even those who by reason of use have their senses exercised to discern both good and evil* (Hebrews 5:13-14, KJV).

When student police officers are training at the police academy, it's mandatory that each one spends an ample amount of time at target practice. During these target practices, the officers are trained to fire a gun at a standing or moving target. The purpose of this exercise is to make sure that the officers have a good command over their weapon and to increase their accuracy at hitting the target.

So many Christians are shooting aimlessly into the spirit world and causing spiritual casualties. Sometimes they hit the target, but it is more by accident than skill. The apostle Paul addressed this in his discourse to the Hebrews, when he declared that those Christians who feed on spiritual milk lack the maturity or skill to discern between good and evil. These believers, no matter how zealous and sincere, are no different from natural babies whose mothers are still changing their diapers.

Undiscerning believers are no different from babies.

He said that believers who live on spiritual milk lack the spiritual maturity and spiritual skill to know when to discharge their weaponry into the spirit world from when they should not. They lack the skill and maturity to accurately discern whether an enemy or a friend is confronting them. They cannot distinguish the difference between good and evil. What these young and inexperienced believers need is to seek the counsel and mentoring of mature believers and prayer warriors who have a proven testimony of walking in the power of God.

These established believers would help to sharpen and perfect the fighting skills of those who are not as seasoned or as spiritually well vested as they are. The spiritual mentoring and the prayer and support of these mature believers will help upcoming spiritual warriors learn to identify the true enemy and aim accurately against the powers of darkness. Mentoring then becomes the impetus that will begin to release the warrior within, the warrior hidden inside the spirit of every child of God.

KNOWING YOUR REAL TARGET

But he turned, and said unto Peter, Get thee behind me, Satan: thou art an offence unto me: for thou savourest not the things that be of God, but those that be of men (Matthew 16:23, KJV).

We have already mentioned that one of the most tragic deaths is the death of a soldier at the receiving end of friendly fire as a result of mistaken identity. Knowing the enemy combatant or the target of attack is crucial before launching any military or spiritual assault. For example, when jet fighters are given a command to go and bomb certain strategic enemy sites, they are given the exact coordinates for these sites. Why? The last thing the government of the United Sates wants is to be accused of dropping bombs on innocent civilians.

The clearest biblical example of distinguishing between an enemy and an ally is found in the passage just quoted, which relates to how the Lord Jesus dealt with Peter. When Peter heard Jesus talking about how He was going to be handed over to the Gentiles to suffer and to be killed, Peter reprimanded Jesus for saying such things.

The Lord Jesus Christ, on the other hand, sharply rebuked Peter for allowing Satan to speak through him. Jesus identified who was really speaking to Him through Peter. When He told Peter, *"Get thee behind me, Satan,"* He was not calling the apostle Peter, "Satan." He was instead identifying who was really speaking through Peter. This is a very important lesson because sometimes the devil will speak or come against you through people you may be acquainted with. You must not begin to think that those people are your spiritual enemies. They are just being used as pawns by a deceptive devil that wants us to focus our energy on fighting people rather than fighting him.

For we wrestle not against flesh and blood, but against principal-

ities, against powers, against the rulers of the darkness of this world, against spiritual wickedness in high places (Ephesians 6:12, KJV).

Paul's epistle to the Ephesians is regarded as one of the most spiritual writings of all his letters. It was in Ephesus that the apostle Paul experienced the greatest revival meeting of his ministry. But it was also in Ephesus that Paul faced his greatest demonic confrontation. There a demoniac beat naked the seven sons of Sceva who had tried to imitate Paul's authentic deliverance ministry.

When the demon-possessed man thrashed the seven sons of Sceva who were practicing magic, it had such an impact on the people in Ephesus that many of them quit practicing witchcraft from that moment on. These are the people whom Paul was addressing in the Book of Ephesians. He knew that since they had already been exposed to demonic activity, they would have a better understanding of the spirit world than other disciples of Christ.

In his discourse to the saints at Ephesus, Paul made it clear that believers do not fight flesh and blood. He told them that we believers actually fight demonic entities or personalities in the spirit world. Paul identified several different types and ranks of these diabolical personalities. He listed these evil entities in order of their spiritual rank in the kingdom of darkness.

Principalities
Powers
Rulers of the darkness of this world
Spiritual wickedness in high places

Principalities are the highest ranking of evil spirits in the satanic kingdom. Satan himself belongs to this rank of spirits, serving as the chief principality. The word *principality* is made of two important words that reveal their rank. It's made of the words *prince* and *pality*. A prince is one who rules over a kingdom, while a "pality" speaks of geography.

A principality therefore is a ruling prince demon, one that governs a large sphere or territory on behalf of the kingdom of darkness. Demonic entities are always the real target of our aggressive warfare, never people. So in order for us to become effective warriors, we must do warfare in the heavens before we can claim a real sense of victory here on the earth.

THE POWER OF SPEAKING IN TONGUES

For he that speaketh in an unknown tongue speaketh not unto men, but unto God: for no man understandeth him; howbeit in the spirit he speaketh mysteries (1 Corinthians 14:2, KJV).

Throughout my Christian walk, I have noticed that praying in tongues has been the most effective method in dealing with the enemy. According to this passage, speaking in tongues first and foremost eliminates the temptation to fight with your flesh. When you pray in tongues, you do not speak or address people; instead, you acquire immediate attention from the living God. When you pray in tongues, your spirit makes a clear one-on-one connection with God.

Secondly, when you pray in tongues, your spirit is speaking a secret, hidden spiritual language that Satan cannot decipher. One of the reasons many believers do not receive favorable results when they pray is that they do not spend enough time praying in tongues. They pray too much with the understanding or the languages of mankind. Satan hears and understands those prayers, and he often maneuvers against their prayers.

Praying in tongues is an effective tool against the enemy.

During war, opposing nations go to great lengths to create a secret code that cannot be easily interpreted by the intelligence of the warring nation. In the event that the enemy intercepts the communications of the different branches of the military of the nations at war, they will not be able to create any military maneuvers because they will not understand the language being used.

On the other hand, if they manage to decipher or unlock the coded communications of their enemy, they would be able to offer countermeasures to the military maneuvers of the other nation. Praying in tongues perplexes the devil; he goes into confusion mode. Much as a rabbit or a deer scurries away in fright when it catches sight of car headlights at night, the devil runs swiftly when he catches the light of our communication in tongues.

> *Likewise the Spirit also helpeth our infirmities: for we know not what we should pray for as we ought: but the Spirit itself maketh intercession for us with groanings which cannot be uttered. And he that searcheth the hearts knoweth what is the mind of the Spirit, because he maketh intercession for the saints according to the will of God*
>
> (Romans 8:26-27, KJV).

The third and probably the most significant benefit of praying in tongues is that it releases us into the ministry of intercession. The verses of Romans 8:26-27 let us know that when we pray in tongues, we activate the mantle of the Holy Spirit who lives inside us. The Bible tells us that the Holy Spirit knows the will and mind of God both for our lives and for every situation that will ever face us.

The Holy Spirit has never failed to hit the target when He is in charge of a spiritual assault against the powers of hell. Can you imagine being led into the battlefield by a commander who never misses a shot no matter how far away the enemy is? Militaries around the world would pay dearly to have a master gunman on their staff, one known for never missing a shot, never missing the target.

You too can access this dimension of the Holy Spirit through praying in tongues. And when you pray in tongues, you begin to build spiritual stamina through the power of the Holy Ghost. At some point in your walk with the Lord Jesus Christ you will need to make a withdrawal of that power. Speaking in tongues will keep your supply high.

But ye, beloved, building up yourselves on your most holy faith, praying in the Holy Ghost (Jude 20, KJV).

PRAYING THE WORD

Then saith Jesus unto him, Get thee hence, Satan: for it is written, Thou shalt worship the Lord thy God, and him only shalt thou serve. Then the devil leaveth him, and, behold, angels came and ministered unto him (Matthew 4:10-11, KJV).

There has never been, neither will there ever be, a spiritual warrior like the Lord Jesus Christ. Christ Jesus never lost a battle. You will do well to imitate His example and learn His warfare tactics. Jesus' most radical confrontation with Satan was at the beginning of His earthly ministry, just after His baptism by John the Baptist.

The Bible tells us that after Jesus was baptized, the heavens were opened and the Holy Spirit descended from heaven like a dove. Jesus was then led into the wilderness by God to be tempted by the devil. The writers of the synoptic gospels graciously recorded the history of this powerful confrontation between the forces of darkness and the kingdom of light.

The Bible says that Satan appeared at the end of Jesus' 40-day fast when He was hungry and began to tempt Him. With each blow that Satan threw at Him, Jesus replied or struck back by saying, "It is written, it is written, it is written." Jesus used the Word as ammunition against the devil. At the end of the confrontation Satan was reeling in defeat, and Jesus descended from the mountain saturated in victory and in the power of the Holy Spirit.

When dealing with the enemy, Jesus left an extraordinary example for every spiritual warrior to follow. Jesus showed us not only how to pray, but also how to speak the Word of God in the midst of heated warfare. Every time and any time that we use God's Word in prayer, we hit the devil right between the eyes. The devil is not afraid of our opinions or college degrees. No, what terrifies him the most is when we access the wonder-working power in the Word of God.

The Scriptures tell us that God's Word is forever established and settled in heaven. So when we speak God's Word, we cannot be defeated. It's practically impossible. Please remember that the world and all that is in it was created by the Word of God. That includes the devil. This is why every-thing in creation has to obey the Word of the living God. The more you use the Word of God in your everyday life, the more it becomes a living reality to you. So you grow from merely speaking the Word into becoming an actual product of the Word that you speak. Speak the Word!

Everything in creation must obey the Word of God!

THE POWER OF PROPHETIC DECREES

Thou shalt also decree a thing, and it shall be established unto thee: and the light shall shine upon thy ways (Job 22:28, KJV).

Another form of warfare prayer that you can use when you pray is the making of prophetic decrees. A decree is a powerful govern-mental word that is more commonly used in a kingdom than in a democracy. In a kingdom the decree of the reigning king or queen becomes the law of the land. If the king or queen decrees that some-one must die, that person can never appeal to anybody else because there is no one of higher authority than the king in any kingdom.

I truly believe that one of the reasons many Christians are failing to hit the target in warfare is that they know how to pray, but few know how to boldly release prophetic decrees into the realms of the spirit. The Bible says that we have been made to sit in heavenly places in Christ Jesus far above all principalities and powers and over everything that is named in this world.

If you visited Buckingham Palace in Great Britain, you would see a portrait of the Queen of England sitting, while her husband is standing and holding her hand. Why are they positioned in this way? The reason is simple but very profound, and has serious governmental implications. The reason the Queen of England is depicted seated on the throne of Great Britain while her husband stands is that she is the reigning monarch. Her husband is simply her helpmate.

The picture shows that Queen Elizabeth is of a higher rank in the kingdom than her husband. She is the head of the kingdom, while he is not. When her husband makes an announcement over the kingdom, it will be received simply as an announcement. But when she makes an announcement, it immediately becomes a decree because she sits on the throne of the kingdom.

The Bible says that when Jesus rose from the dead and went back to heaven He took us with Him, and when He sat on the throne of the kingdom, we sat with Him. If we adopt the heavenly perspective in our spiritual warfare model, we will begin to see that we are truly raised to reign with Christ in the heavens far above Satan's headquarters in the second heaven. If we are really seated with Christ, we can then begin to make prophetic decrees with the authority of the King. Glory to God in the highest!

CHAPTER EIGHT

DEFEATING YOUR ENEMY THROUGH PRAYER AND PRAISE

Elias was a man subject to like passions as we are, and he prayed earnestly that it might not rain: and it rained not on the earth by the space of three years and six months (James 5:17, KJV).

WHAT IS PRAYER?

There is nothing more universal in human history than prayer. It is practiced in nearly every culture and language. It is the common denominator of every world religion. Whether someone is Buddhist, Hindu, Muslim, or Christian, there seems to be a fundamental agreement in the human spirit about the utter importance of prayer as it relates to a life of faith.

Prayer is even more potent for the Christian who understands that he or she is praying to the true and living God. Unfortunately, because of time restraints, few believers take advantage of the power of prayer. When you do not pray, you will not have a guarded life. This is why most Christians fail to fully release the warrior within; they have not yet made a serious commitment to the business of praying.

Most of the greatest heroes of the faith in the Bible totally relied on the power of prayer to overcome the powers of hell. One example of this is the patriarch Abraham. He prayed for Abimelech and his entire household after God judged them because Abimelech had taken Sarah, Abraham's wife, for himself. After Abraham prayed, the Lord healed Abimelech and his entire household.

When Isaac saw that his wife Rebekah was barren, he prayed to God for her. The Lord healed her and she was able to conceive children. The Bible explicitly reports what happened at the dedication of King Solomon's temple. After Solomon had finished praying, the fire of God fell and His glory filled the temple in such a way that the Levitical priests could not minister. The temple was flooded with the power and presence of God.

> *Now when Solomon had made an end of praying, the fire came down from heaven, and consumed the burnt offering and the sacrifices; and the glory of the LORD filled the house* (2 Chronicles 7:1, KJV).

The connection between prayer and the release of God's supernatural power to destroy the yokes of the enemy is highly unmistakable. I could go on and on giving multiple examples of how God answered the prayers of His people both in the Scriptures and today. There would be enough accounts to literally fill up thousands of volumes of books. So exactly what is prayer and why is it so important in defeating your enemy? This is the question of all questions. Best-selling author and Bible teacher Dr. Myles Munroe gives an adequate answer to this question in his book, *Understanding the Purpose and Power of Prayer*. He says:

> Prayer is man giving God the legal right and permission to intervene in earth's affairs.
> Prayer is man giving heaven earthly license to influence earth.
> Prayer is a terrestrial license for celestial interference.
> Prayer is man exercising his legal authority on earth to invoke heaven's influence on the planet.[1]

These definitions of prayer make it clear that you cannot defeat the devil and his host of demons without engaging in warfare prayer. When you pray, you are permitting God to move on your behalf. When you pray, you are summoning the supernatural ministry of God's warring angels who come to war on your behalf. Nothing can help you to release the warrior within like a dedicated life of prayer.

PRAYER AND FASTING

When Jesus saw that the people came running together, he rebuked the foul spirit, saying unto him, Thou dumb and deaf spirit, I charge thee, come out of him, and enter no more into him....And he said unto them, This kind can come forth by nothing, but by prayer and fasting (Mark 9:26,29, KJV).

The Lord Jesus Christ had taken His three closest disciples, Peter, John, and James, to the Mount of Transfiguration, while the rest of the apostles remained in the valley below. On the mountain Jesus was gloriously transfigured right before His baffled and deeply awed disciples as He spoke with Moses and Elijah about His coming death and resurrection. Afterward, a desperate father came to the disciples, bringing his teenage son who was deeply oppressed by a deaf and dumb spirit.

This man desperately wanted his son to be healed. Since Jesus was unavailable at the time, he turned to the disciples to see if they could cast the devil out of the boy and heal him. All their attempts to cast the demon out of the child were futile. While this was happening, Jesus and the other three disciples were coming down from the Mount of Transfiguration.

The father then ran to Jesus and begged Him to deliver his ailing son. Jesus quickly commanded the deaf and dumb spirit to leave the boy's body. Amazingly, the demon left him and the boy received his healing. Hours later the apostles, who were very disappointed at their inability to cast out this particular devil, finally mustered the courage to ask the Lord Jesus why they had not been able to cast the demon out. Jesus replied, *"This kind can come forth by nothing, but by prayer and fasting"* (KJV).

We have already concluded that prayer is very powerful. But from this passage of Scripture we see that fasting is one of the most powerful accessories to prayer. In chapter 58 of the Book of Isaiah, the Bible declares that if we pray and fast, God will supernaturally destroy the yoke of the enemy in our lives and in the lives of others. He also promised that if we fast and pray, He will supernaturally break the bands of wickedness from our lives.

After Jesus was baptized, He was led by the Spirit of God into the wilderness. While in the wilderness, the Spirit of God led Jesus to pray and fast for 40 days. In the Book of Luke, we read that Jesus returned in the fullness of the power of the Holy Ghost. *"And Jesus returned in the power of the Spirit into Galilee: and there went out a fame of him through all the region round about* (Luke 4:14, KJV). Jesus was so filled with the power of God from His time of praying and fasting that from that time of intimacy spent with God He immediately launched His worldwide ministry of healing and deliverance.

Fasting is one of the most powerful accessories to prayer. In the Book of Daniel we find that Daniel was in a serious time of praying and fasting for three straight weeks (Daniel 10). He was hungry to see a move of God in his life and to see God deliver the people of Israel from Babylonian captivity. For 21 days he travailed in prayer and caused tremendous commotion in the spirit realm. Daniel did not actually realize just how much his time of prayer and fasting was dismantling ancient demonic strongholds. His prayers were even challenging the authority of the demonic prince of Persia—the principality that ruled the entire region of Persia.

There are some things that can be overcome simply by praying. But when you realize that your prayers are not actually getting the results that you desire, or perhaps the demons that you are confronting are age-old demons that refuse to leave since they believe they have the right to stay, then you may need to combine your prayer with fasting. Combining prayer with fasting always gets miraculous results. To learn more about prayer and fasting and how to properly do it, I recommend reading Mahesh Chavda's book, *The Hidden Power of Prayer and Fasting* (Destiny Image Publishers) or Marilyn Hickey's *The Power of Prayer and Fasting: 21 Days That Can Change Your Life* (Warner Faith Books).

THE PRAYER OF FAITH

And the prayer of faith shall save the sick, and the Lord shall raise him up; and if he have committed sins, they shall be forgiven him (James 5:15, KJV).

A thorough examination of the Scriptures will quickly reveal that there are different types of prayers in the Bible, depending on the need. There is the prayer of petition, the prayer of repentance, the prayer or supplication, the prayer of intercession, and so forth. However, one of the most powerful prayers we can ever pray is the one the apostle James calls the prayer of faith. Why is the prayer of faith so powerful in totally annihilating the powers of the enemy?

As its name suggests, this is a prayer that is saturated with the spirit of faith. The Bible is very clear that without faith it is impossible to please God, because God only responds to faith. He never responds to need. This is because God's greatest desire is to be believed and trusted by His people. Jesus also said that nothing shall be impossible for those who believe. Faith is the supernatural hand of the spirit that reaches out to God and receives what He has promised. Faith refuses to reach out, yet come back empty-handed.

When the prophet Elijah prayed that there would be no rain for three years, he did not pray weak prayers. He prayed the prayer of faith. Nothing can release the warrior within like praying the word of faith. Every spiritual exploit that our spiritual forefathers performed was accomplished by the operation of the spirit of faith. When you function by the spirit of faith in your prayers, you join yourself to the spiritual legacy of the forefathers and access the unlimited power of God.

A LOOK AT PRAISE

Let every thing that hath breath praise the LORD. Praise ye the LORD (Psalm 150:6, KJV).

This weapon of praise is not merely an effective warfare weapon; it also is a command from God. Neither is this command limited to humans. Rather, it is a command to everything in the universe that has life—including the animal kingdom, vegetable kingdom, and minerals. When Jesus entered Jerusalem riding on a donkey's back, men, women, and children began to praise the Lord, shouting, *"Blessed is He who comes in the name of the LORD!"* (Matthew 21:9) When the Pharisees heard this, they were very angry and demanded that Jesus command the people to stop praising Him.

Jesus explained that if the people stopped praising Him, God would cause the very stones to praise Him (Luke 19:40). This is how powerful the weapon of praise is. It can bring life to situations that have been marred with death. One of the Hebrew words for praise is *shabach*, which carries the meaning of addressing someone in a loud tone of voice.[2] This means that we cannot effectively use the weapon of praise without opening our mouths. When we start to praise God, we are simply declaring and speaking into the spirit world what we know to be true about God. Spiritual warriors who understand the praise principle know that whenever God's people praise Him, they literally terrorize the devil in the process.

Praisers inundate the Lord with words of adoration and exaltation. Can you imagine what will happen to every demon hiding in your life when the atmosphere around you is saturated with faith-filled words of adoration such as, "The Lord is good"; "God is worthy"; "God is holy"; and "God is a miracle-working God"? An atmosphere saturated with words such as those will flush out bad spirits from your life. This is why Satan doesn't want you to live a life of praise.

The Hebrew word *shabach* also carries the meaning of speaking pacifying words to someone.[3] This concept of praise carries the meaning of the work of an accomplished lawyer as he stands to defend his client before a judge. The job of a good lawyer is to rally the right words that will form a pacifying argument before the judge, swaying the jury toward making a favorable verdict on behalf of his client. When we put on the weapon of praise, we are like lawyers appearing before the Lord, who is the Judge of the whole earth, to argue our cases so God can rule in our favor. Every time God rules in our favor, He destroys the powers of hell and releases miracles into our lives.

Praise is so powerful, it can bring life to situations that have been marred with death.

This is how we praise the Lord…

PRAISE HIM WITH INSTRUMENTS

Praise him with the sound of the trumpet: praise him with the psaltery and harp. Praise him with the timbrel and dance: praise him with stringed instruments and organs. Praise him upon the loud cymbals: praise him upon the high sounding cymbals (Psalm 150:3-5, KJV).

PRAISE HIM WITH DANCING

Let them praise his name in the dance: let them sing praises unto him with the timbrel and harp (Psalm 149:3, KJV).

PRAISE HIM WITH THE LIPS AND SONG

By him therefore let us offer the sacrifice of praise to God continually, that is, the fruit of our lips giving thanks to his name (Hebrews 13:15, KJV).

PRAISE HIM WITH GIVING

Do not forget or neglect to do kindness and good, to be generous and distribute and contribute to the needy [of the church as embodiment and proof of fellowship], for such sacrifices are pleasing to God (Hebrews 13:16, AMP).

THE BATTLE BELONGS TO THE LORD

And when he had consulted with the people, he appointed singers unto the LORD, and that should praise the beauty of holiness, as they went out before the army, and to say, Praise the LORD; for his mercy endureth for ever. And when they began to sing and to praise, the LORD set ambushments against the children of Ammon, Moab, and mount Seir, which were come against Judah; and they were smitten (2 Chronicles 20:21-22, KJV).

King Jehoshaphat was facing a national crisis when he received reports from his military intelligence that the nations of Moab and Seir had brought thousands of men of war to the borders of Israel and were preparing to fight with the Israelites. The sheer numbers of their armies was mind-boggling and terrified King Jehoshaphat. But then King Jehoshaphat did what every godly leader should do in periods of crisis.

He called for a nationwide time of prayer and fasting to the living God. It was during this time of fasting and praying that God sent a prophet to King Jehoshaphat. The prophet told him not to worry. He said that the battle belonged to the Lord and that God was going to fight on Jehoshaphat's behalf. All he had to do was to continually give God the praise. King Jehoshaphat obeyed the prophet and gave instructions for a company of singers and musicians to go ahead of the military as they praised their way into the battle.

Could you imagine what would happen if the President of the United States placed singers and musicians in front of the Marines or the Air Force during a war? He would be impeached immediately and laughed to scorn. But this is exactly what King Jehoshaphat did. His enemies must have found it very comical and absurd when they saw the armies of Israel hiding behind singers and musicians; but God uses the foolish things of this world to confuse the wise. They thought this fight was going to be an easy one, but they were wrong. King Jehoshaphat was employing a very potent weapon— the ancient weapon of praise.

This same weapon has proven to defeat the enemy over and over again. It worked then and it still works now. Abraham, Isaac, Jacob, Moses, King David—all used praise many times to get the victory. The Bible says that while the enemy scorned them, God thundered out of the heavens and terrified their enemies. The invading armies were so confused and terrified that they turned on each other and began to kill one another while the Israelites stood by and watched.

After the battle, there was a river of blood in the fields where the enemy had once been. King Jehoshaphat and his army just stood there. They had never lifted a finger to fight It suddenly dawned on them that they had never been intended to fight this battle in the first place. This battle was the Lord's! You praise and let God fight. The more you praise God, the more you'll fuel Him to fight on your behalf.

GOD INHABITS THE PRAISES OF HIS PEOPLE

But thou art holy, O thou that inhabitest the praises of Israel (Psalm 22:3, KJV).

Your praise creates a supernatural highway that the throne of God travels on. When you start to praise God, His throne moves to your location. Wherever you are, that place literally becomes the throne room. A courtroom is really not a courtroom until the judge enters in. That is why the bailiff is there to watch for the entrance of the judge. As soon as the judge enters the courtroom, the bailiff instructs everyone in the room to rise while the judge walks in. Once the judge is seated, the bailiff then announces, "Court is now in session, the honorable judge now presiding."

You see, the building doesn't make the court; the judges make the court. If the legal proceedings were transferred to a school hall, then the moment the judge walked into it and took his seat, that school hall would suddenly be transformed into a courtroom with all the attending rights and privileges. Any judgments or sentences passed by the judge in that school hall would be binding by law. This is what happens when we enter into praise. Our praise relocates the seat of the heavenly Judge to wherever we are. Once He arrives there and takes His seat, wherever we are is suddenly transformed into the mercy seat.

Our praise relocates the seat of the heavenly judge to wherever we are.

Every angel assigned to guard the mercy seat or throne of God is also relocated to where we are. I hope you are grasping the power of this revelation. Imagine having the power to convene a court session with the living God in your own living room or workplace, so

He can pass sentence on every demon that's contesting His precious promises in your life. That's exactly what happens each and every time you praise the Lord; the Judge comes in and rules favorably on your behalf.

Endnotes
1. Myles Munroe, *Understanding the Purpose and Power of Prayer* (New Kensington, Pennsylvania: Whitaker House, 2002).
2. James Strong, *The Exhaustive Concordance of the Bible* (Nashville, Tennessee: Holman Bible Publishers, n.d.), #H7623.
3. *Ibid.*

CHAPTER NINE

USING SEEDS AS AMMUNITION

And a certain centurion's servant, who was dear unto him, was sick, and ready to die. And when he heard of Jesus, he sent unto him the elders of the Jews, beseeching him that he would come and heal his servant. And when they came to Jesus, they besought him instantly, saying, That he was worthy for whom he should do this: For he loveth our nation, and he hath built us a synagogue (Luke 7:2-5, KJV).

The "planting of seed" or "giving" is yet another warfare strategy we can use against the enemy. When the Roman centurion's servant was attacked with a life-threatening illness, he sent some of the chief elders of Israel to Jesus to see if they could get the Lord to heal his beloved servant. When the elders of Israel got to Jesus, they stated this man's case before Him. In his defense, the elders were quick to emphasize that this Roman centurion had earned the right to receive a miracle from God.

The basis of their argument was that this man had sown a seed into the nation of Israel by building them a synagogue. The elders used his sacrificial seed as the basis for their argument—that if anybody deserved a chance at receiving miraculous intervention, this was the man. What really excites me about this story is that Jesus did not make an attempt to correct their theology, and we know from Scripture that Jesus had zero tolerance for wrong doctrine.

He was quick to shoot down wrong doctrine. But in this case He accepted the reasoning of the elders. Jesus healed the man's servant. The healing of his servant was the fruit of the centurion's harvest for seed he had previously sown. This story clearly proves that as God's spiritual warriors, we can use our financial seeds to overcome the powers of the enemy that have rallied against us. So in this chapter we will look at other examples of how Bible greats used the power of the seed sown to effect major change in their lives. Having said this, we first need to briefly understand how the principle of seedtime and harvest time operates.

SEEDTIME AND HARVEST TIME

While the earth remaineth, seedtime and harvest, and cold and heat, and summer and winter, and day and night shall not cease (Genesis 8:22, KJV).

Both the spiritual and the natural worlds are governed by a set of spiritual and natural laws. These governing laws cannot be changed or ignored. They affect us all, whether or not we believe in them. One of these laws is a dual law that has both spiritual and physical ramifications. This law is the immutable law of seedtime and harvest. God gave this law to Noah after he and his sons survived the flood. According to God, this law would always remain in effect as long as the earth remains. This means that as long as anyone can see, touch, and walk on this earth, this law will never cease to work.

According to this law, if you sow a seed here on earth, whether that seed is spiritual or financial, you will reap a harvest of what you have previously sown. If you sow an apple seed, you'll reap a harvest of an apple tree with apples on its branches. If you sow love, you will reap love in return. If you sow cars, you will reap a harvest of automobiles. If you sow money, you actually receive more than money in return, since money represents your life.

You actually receive life back in return. It even works in the negative. Sowing negative and evil seeds will unleash seasons of personal pain and tragedy. These evil seeds have the power to open the portals of hell into your life until it has become a treading ground for every foul spirit. For example, the seed of stinginess will usually unleash a spirit of poverty and lack against our lives.

Whatever you sow— whether positive or negative— you will reap in return.

King Saul consistently sowed the seed of disobedience to God; as a result, his life torpedoed into spiritual destruction. He lost his mantle as God's spiritual warrior because he constantly sowed seeds that shut the doors of heaven and unlocked hell. This is why it's critical for us to understand how this law works; it not only affects our warfare but also has the ability to delay the release of God's Spirit in our life.

YOUR SEED—AN EARLY PHOTO OF YOUR FAITH

But this I say, He which soweth sparingly shall reap also sparingly; and he which soweth bountifully shall reap also bountifully (2 Corinthians 9:6, KJV).

Your seeds, whether they are spiritual or financial, become photographs of your faith. God has a serious obsession with faith. In God's dealings with man, nothing changes until somebody uses his or her faith. The Lord only rewards those who diligently seek Him enough to believe Him. Faith is a product of the human spirit, so it's practically invisible to the natural eye, except through the corresponding actions that accompany its expression. This is why the

Bible says, *"For as the body without the spirit is dead, so faith without works is dead also"* (James 2:26). This is why God watches the sowing of uncommon financial seeds; they are indicators that the hand of faith is reaching out to touch God.

> *And the king said unto Araunah, Nay; but I will surely buy it of thee at a price: neither will I offer burnt offerings unto the LORD my God of that which doth cost me nothing. So David bought the threshingfloor and the oxen for fifty shekels of silver. And David built there an altar unto the LORD, and offered burnt offerings and peace offerings. So the LORD was entreated for the land, and the plague was stayed from Israel* (2 Samuel 24:24-25, KJV).

King David stopped a death angel that had slain more than 70,000 of his people. At the height of this angelic invasion upon the nation of Israel—caused by King David's sin of having numbered the people—David went to see a man called Araunah to see if he could buy his threshing floor. He wanted to sacrifice to the Lord there before the entire nation was wiped out.

Araunah was more than happy to give his threshing floor to King David at no cost to him at all, but David refused. David knew that he was in a serious spiritual battle and that he needed an outside point of contact that would help focus his faith toward releasing a breakthrough—one that would cause God to stay the angel of death. King David knew that uncommon seeds, sown in moments of great spiritual battles, would create uncommon miracles of intervention.

David told Araunah that he would not give to God something that cost him nothing. That is a lesson that many people in the church really need to understand. You can't bring your junk to God and expect Him to receive it. After you've shopped for clothes, gone to the movies, bought groceries, and ordered things online, whatever is left over you then give to God. That's crazy! God deserves the best seed, which is always the first fruit of all your increase. God always requires the best that you have. Anything less than your best is an unworthy sacrifice.

David knew that through his sacrificial giving he would direct his hands of faith to lay hold of the mercy seat of God. David gave his special offering to the Lord and worshipped, and God instructed the angel of death to stop the massacre of Israel. Your seed has amazing ability to transform your life and the lives of others. Your seed can literally save lives. In God's eye your seed and you are identical twins. God does not see your flesh, only your faith. That's why your seeds are personal photographs sent to heaven of what you look like and how much you are growing in God here on earth.

SEEDS OF FAITH-FILLED WORDS

Then said he unto me, Fear not, Daniel: for from the first day that thou didst set thine heart to understand, and to chasten thyself before thy God, thy words were heard, and I am come for thy words (Daniel 10:12, KJV).

Anything God wants, He creates with His words. He literally speaks them into being. When God created the world, He used faith-filled words that He spoke into the darkness. When He wanted light, He spoke into the darkness and the seeds of His glorious light were sown—and light appeared! Words are very important to God. If they are filled with faith, they release His power and presence. If they are filled with doubt and unbelief, they unravel His power and presence, unleashing the hordes of hell. The closer a person walks with God, the more he or she becomes very careful of what words he or she uses.

Faith-filled words release God's power and presence.

People are moved by words. Marriages are enacted through

words. Great world-shaking visions are cast with words. Presidents rise and fall on the basis of their power of persuasion. In the court-room, innocent men and women are wrongly imprisoned because their defending attorney didn't present an effective legal argument to the jury. In other words, the jury did not believe the words of the defending attorney. All business contracts written or spoken are simply a lot of words.

Furthermore, contracts worth billions of dollars are signed each day on the basis of an agreement of words that have been typed out. Words are powerful. To ignore this fact will seriously injure our ability to become effective warriors for Christ. In order to fully release the spiritual warrior within, we must respect the awesome power of faith-filled words. Faith-filled words are powerful seeds that we can sow into the spirit realm to create a harvest of miracles.

Angels are moved by words. Demons and devils are moved by words. When we cast out devils, we do not cast them out in silence. We cast them out with faith-filled words. The Bible says that the people of Jesus' day were astonished at His doctrine because He was different from the Pharisees and Sadducees. He taught and spoke like one who had authority, and He cast out evil spirits with His words. This is what got the attention of the masses—the power and authority of His words.

When the angel appeared to Daniel, he told him that he had been sent from the throne of God because of Daniel's spoken words. His words had caused God to dispatch this powerful angel! The angel told Daniel that his words were creating serious confronta-tions between the angels of God and Satan's fallen angels. What are your words creating? Are your words killing demons and causing new life to happen? Or are your words further perpetuating a crisis? Whatever you say, you become an owner of. To that end, be careful of what you say.

Thou art snared with the words of thy mouth, thou art taken with the words of thy mouth (Proverbs 6:2, KJV).

THE WIDOW WHO CHEATED DEATH

There is another prophetic portrayal of a warrior who discovered the power of her seed. Her story is recorded in First Kings 17. The account of this widow is a classic example of how a seed sown can actually reverse the curse of poverty on one's life. The word of the Lord came to the prophet Elijah, informing him to go to a widow's house. When Elijah arrived at the gates of the city of Zarephath, the woman was there at the city gates gathering sticks, expecting to prepare her final meal before she died.

First the prophet asked her to go get a cup of water for him. But in a moment he changed his mind and obeyed God; as she went to get the water, the prophet told her to also prepare him a meal. The principle here is that you should never give anything to a man or woman of God that costs you nothing. After hearing the prophet's request, she became very afraid. Why would a world-renowned prophet ask her for her last meal in the midst of an apparent crisis? Because she respected the office of the prophet, although she did not understand why he would make such a demand, she eventually agreed. Perhaps she knew that God was trying to position her for a miracle.

Before she agreed, though, she began to tell Elijah how bad things were in her life and how the ingredients that she had were not enough to feed unexpected company, just herself and her son. She was hoping that the prophet would release her from this request. But what she didn't know was that the prophet had the ability to cause her life to flourish once again—if only she would obey.

To add insult to injury, her son was already sick and close to death. Barring a miracle, he was going to die anyway. Things always get bleaker when the spirit of poverty invites the spirit of death to join the party. Her logic was that the only thing standing between her and sure death was the last piece of meal that she was preparing to eat that day.

I'm sure she was hoping that when she painted a picture of her problems, he would feel sorry for her and apologize for even asking. The prophet Elijah, though, was on a divine assignment to show her that, as helpless as she was feeling, she still had in her arsenal a very lethal spiritual weapon that she had not yet used: the seed.

The spirit of fear comes for one reason: to paralyze your faith. That's why the prophet rebuked the spirit of fear from her, causing holy boldness to rise within her so that she could obey God. The primary reason people have financial challenges is that they are afraid. They live in constant fear of what might happen if they sow a seed and then a bill or expense suddenly comes due. Their fear causes them not to sow, leaving them in the same predicament they were in from the very beginning.

The man of God gave the widow a prophetic portrait of the supernatural harvest awaiting her on the other side of her obedience. He told her that her seed would unlock heaven's storehouses and flood her life with never-ending abundance. One seed sown would eradicate her lack and chase poverty away forever. If one seed sown can cause this kind of miracle to happen, consider what would happen if many seeds are sown!

If only one seed sown can cause a miracle, what would happen if many seeds were sown?

Both the widow and her son had very urgent appointments with death. Most people never cheat death. But she did. Interestingly, Jesus also cheated death: He became alive again! But He could not cheat death until He became a seed for us. A seed is a forceful weapon of warfare that literally cancels death appointments and brings prosperity and wholeness.

When the widow believed the words of the prophet, she realized that her situation would only get better. Like a guided missile, she released her weapon of a seed into the arms of God, and the rest is history. The Bible says that immediately there was a supernatural, limitless supply of flour and oil. Her supply would never fail. Just think, she'd had nothing but one cake. But after she gave that cake away, she had an enterprise. Soon the entire city of Zarephath was hovering over her house with outstretched hands. The weapon of her seed had not only driven the devil out of her life, but had also driven the devil out of her city. A spiritual warrior was born.

DESTROYING THE SPIRIT OF BARRENNESS

The Shunammite woman and her husband were people of high standing in the society in which they lived. (See Second Kings 4.) Because of their influence, Satan caused a spirit of barrenness to close her womb so that her godly heritage would not continue on through their loins. During that time, women were not actively involved in the workforce and in politics as they are today, so they made their name great primarily through giving their husband children—plenty of children.

This couple had a public image of success, but privately they nursed serious pain and disappointment. Although she enjoyed success and status, she would have traded it all just to give birth to a baby. Then there came a day when the prophet Elisha passed by her house, and she invited him to come into her house and stay. Her husband made a room for the prophet, adding more space in which he could live comfortably. Allowing the prophet to stay in her home and caring for his needs was a seed sown into the prophet's life.

After Elisha had moved in, he asked the Shunammite woman what she wanted, for he wanted to bless her for her kindness. He wanted to know what she desired as a harvest. She was taken by surprise by the prophet's request because she had not been expecting anything in exchange for her generosity. Gehazi, Elisha's servant, told the prophet that the Shunammite woman was barren and that she and her husband longed to have a child of their own.

The prophet of God told her that her seed canceled the power of barrenness over her body and opened her womb. The prophet also told her that within a year she would give birth to a male child—an honor for those times. True to his word, within a year she became a mother. Her seed actually stopped the spirit of barrenness and caused life to come forth.

SEED—A MEMORIAL UNTO THE LORD

And when he looked on him, he was afraid, and said, What is it, Lord? And he said unto him, Thy prayers and thine alms are come up for a memorial before God (Acts 10:4, KJV).

Imagine what Cornelius must have felt when his room was invaded by an angelic being as brilliant as the sun. He must have been petrified, wondering what was happening. But the angel did not leave him in suspense very long; he quickly announced his reason for being there. Heaven had sent this angel to let Cornelius know that his prayers and his giving had come before God.

My friend, when was the last time an angel appeared to you to let you know that your prayers and your giving are literally moving the hand of God? This man was not giving little, insignificant offerings. No, he was giving offerings that actually got God's attention. He was giving his absolute best. You say, "It's not the amount. It's the heart behind your giving." That is true, but I can also add that it's not how much you give, but how much you have left after you've given.

If a billionaire gives a $1,000 seed, is that really a gift unto the Lord, or is it an insult? I believe it's an insult. You have to give where you are. You have to sow so substantially that you actually feel that you've given. Those are the kinds of gifts that God recognizes and honors. If someone earns $15,000 annually and sows a $1,000 seed into the ministry, it's quite obvious that they've sown a major portion of their life into the ministry. A billionaire wouldn't be affected after giving a seed of $1,000.

Every time Cornelius prayed, he also sowed a seed. His praying and sowing literally impressed God to the point that, the angel told him, God decided to save his soul and that of his entire family. The angel also told him that his seed would open a door, connecting him with the apostle Peter, a prophetic connection.

I am convinced that we will never see the full actualization or release of the spiritual warrior within until we realize the power that our weapon of the seed has in warfare. Never underestimate the power of sowing a financial seed. It's a weapon rarely used; but when it is, it literally causes a spiritual revolution.

CHAPTER TEN

TAKING IT BY FORCE

And from the days of John the Baptist until now the kingdom of heaven suffereth violence, and the violent take it by force (Matthew 11:12, KJV).

After all that you've read and all the information that you've received, I must end with some important words: *"The violent take it by force."* There is no way you will simply say a few cute words, wave a "magic wand" over your troubles, and watch them go away like hocus pocus. Whatever gains you make in the spirit world will come when you choose to take them by force. After all, we are soldiers in the army of the Lord.

The devil has stolen your most valued possessions, and now he is using them for his own benefit. He does not want to give them back to you freely. If you want to regain your possessions, you can't be nice about it. You are going to have to take them by force. You must be hungry, passionate, and uncompromising concerning pursuing God. If you really love God, your love will be greatly recognized when you won't take "no" for an answer. Your love for Him will be known when you tap into your covenant rights and begin to act as though you have the authority of Christ.

This new prophetic company of spiritual warriors will understand the power and passion of spiritual hunger. Imagine having to be the referee standing between a bag of food and a group of homeless men and women who have not eaten for days. No doubt you would become the victim of a violent stampede when they begin dashing toward the food. Are you beginning to get the picture?

GETTING TRAMPLED AND GETTING BLESSED

The story recorded in Second Kings chapters 6 and 7 illustrates how believers are required to be aggressive about receiving the blessing God promised to them. There was a serious famine in Samaria because the Syrians had placed the city under siege. They would not allow outside traders to enter into the gates of Samaria; neither did they allow the inhabitants of Samaria to have contact with outsiders.

The siege went on for such a long time that the city of Samaria ran out of food. The situation got so bad that mothers were even eating their own children just to stay alive. But things got worse. The king of Israel was so mad that he blamed the prophet Elisha for the siege and vowed to kill him. Before the king and his entourage arrived at the prophet's house, the Lord warned Elisha and prepared him for the ensuing confrontation.

God is looking for people with a passionate hunger for Him.

When the king of Israel and his chief treasurer arrived at the prophet's house, Elisha, under a strong prophetic anointing, prophesied that God was going to restore the shattered economy in Samaria within a space of about 24 hours. Imagine what would happen if a prophet of the Lord prophesied over America that its economy would once again flourish within 24 hours! It would inspire much curiosity about God and His power. Perhaps it would cause some die-hard skeptics to become believers.

136

The king's chief treasurer laughed at what he thought was the prophet's foolish presumptions and began to mock him and the word of the Lord. Elisha responded to the minister of finance, telling him that although he would see the fulfillment of the prophetic word, he would not enjoy the benefits of it. Meanwhile, at the city gates, God was already moving on the hearts of four lepers and gave them a bold and radical ideal.

As they were consulting with one another, God put it in their hearts to go to the camp of the Syrians and see if the Syrians would give them food. Since there was no food in the city, they felt that they would not have much to lose anyway if they went to the enemy. The worst thing that could happen if the Syrians refused to give them food was that they would be killed. And without food they'd die anyway. Either way, the four lepers were tired of sitting at the city gates. When they arrived at the camp of the Syrians, they found that the camp was totally deserted—but all the spoils of war and food that they had been carrying were left behind.

What the Syrians had left in their haste was an abundance of food and precious minerals such as these lepers had never seen. They ran back to Samaria and reported their findings to the king. The king sent a messenger to go and verify their report. When the lepers' report of an abandoned Syrian military camp filled with an abundance of food started to spread, there was a stampede that rocked the foundations of the city as starved men, women, and children ran toward the camp of the Syrians.

The king assigned the treasurer to handle the transportation of the food and jewelry from the camp of the enemy. So the treasurer positioned himself at the gate of the city, where he attempted to stand between the ensuing stampede of starving men and women and the promise of food. This was the wrong thing to do. This unstoppable horde of hungry men and women crushed the chief of the treasury to a pulp.

God is seeking out the kind of warriors who have the same passion as this stampeding army of hungry men and women. God wants people who refuse to take "no" for an answer. When you are going to do things God's way or no way at all, you can't be concerned with who's in your way. Whoever is in your way will just have to get trampled over.

THE CANAANITE WOMAN

And, behold, a woman of Canaan came out of the same coasts, and cried unto him, saying, Have mercy on me, O Lord, thou Son of David; my daughter is grievously vexed with a devil (Matthew 15:22, KJV).

This Canaanite woman came to Jesus in desperate need of a miracle of deliverance. Her only daughter had fallen prey to the devil. Evil and oppressive spirits had taken over this child's life. This grieving mother ran to find Jesus, determined that she was not going to return without a miracle for her troubled child. To her surprise, when she got to Jesus, He blatantly ignored her desperate cries for help.

Many Christians would have given up at the first sign of resistance. They would have concluded that Jesus was not really interested in helping them and walked away. But not so with this woman; she belonged to a different class of fighters. She refused to be denied. She continued crying out to Jesus until it became irritating to the apostles. They turned on her and asked Jesus to send her away. Can you imagine going to a Benny Hinn crusade in search of healing, only to be ignored by Pastor Benny Hinn and then told to leave by his ministry staff? Most folks would not stay around to hear the benediction of the service.

When Jesus finally responded to her, He actually rejected her. He told her that He was not called to people who were not of Jewish heritage. This woman could have left in tears, with justifiable reasons. First Jesus came off as being quite racially berating. Second, He appeared as if He really could not have cared less about her request. One of the things I know for sure is that most people are not very good at handling rejection. Often those who cannot handle rejection are those who typically settle for less in life. The ability to deal with rejection is a hallmark of true spiritual maturity.

> *The ability to deal with rejection is a hallmark of true spiritual maturity.*

The Canaanite woman could have walked away from Jesus in anger, accusing Him of being a racist. But instead she took the slap of His rejection and continued to violently pursue Him. Her daughter's healing was surely worth the fight. On top of that, she knew that Jesus had the ability to successfully get the job done. So what good would it have done if she left angry and offended, without the blessing that she was hoping for?

When Jesus realized her persistence, He attacked her pride by insulting her. He told her that it was not right for Him to give the children's bread to dogs. Just think, Jesus called this woman a dog and suggested that she didn't deserve the blessing she was seeking. Understand that some words may have been culturally and historically relative. But to call someone a dog in this modern era or even then was just as offensive. As some would say, "Those are fighting words." And that's exactly the cue that this woman received when Jesus said this to her. She decided that those words only meant that she would have to fight a little bit harder to get her desire.

He didn't call her a dog privately; rather, He said that in an audience of thousands of witnesses standing on the sidelines waiting and watching to see was going to happen next. Instead of giving up on her miracle, this woman fired back with a statement that simply brought Jesus to a standstill. *"And she said, Truth, Lord: yet the dogs eat of the crumbs which fall from their masters' table"* (Matthew 15:27,

KJV). In other words, if she was a dog, then she was His dog. And He knew that He was still obligated to care for His own pet.

As His dog she could still expect to eat of the crumbs that were falling from His table. Jesus was impressed with her attitude. Her daughter was healed. This is what it means to take it by force. Jesus turned to His baffled apostles and told them that He had never met a person with such great faith in Israel before.

THE WOMAN WITH THE ISSUE OF BLOOD

And a certain woman, which had an issue of blood twelve years...For she said, If I may touch but his clothes, I shall be whole (Mark 5:25, 28, KJV).

The Scriptures contain so many examples of people who exercised violent faith. But I thought it would be best to bring this chapter and book to a close by looking at the persistent faith of the woman with an issue of blood. The text introduces her as a nameless woman. I guess it doesn't really matter what her name was; her violent faith stands far higher than her name. This woman suffered with a hemorrhaging condition for 12 years. She went to the best specialists; she spent all her money trying to get cured; yet she only got worse.

During that time she heard about Jesus. She heard that He would be in the same vicinity where she lived. Although she was ceremonially unclean and should not have been out in public, she was firm about receiving her healing from God. She determined within herself that she was going to fight her way through this massive crowd until she touched the hem of His garment. She knew that, if caught, she could have been stoned to death. Even in her pursuit, she could have been squeezed to death by the crowd.

This woman was like most warriors who live a life where they are already counted as dead; death was not something to fear. By this time she was a societal outcast anyway, so she may have already felt dead, or, even worse, anticipated death. Perhaps without a touch from God she would not want to live at all. Whatever her thought, she made up her mind that it was going to be today or never. She was going to violently press her way through to Jesus. She was going to touch the hem of His garment that day, no matter what.

Just imagine how physically weak you would be if you bled for 12 consecutive years. Despite her weakness, nothing was going to stand between her and Jesus. Put yourself in her shoes. No, don't see yourself as a bleeding, suffering invalid. Don't see yourself as a social outcast. Rather, see yourself as someone who will not be denied, no matter what.

See yourself as someone who will not be denied, no matter what.

My prayer is that you and the rest of the body of Christ will finally realize who you are in Christ. All the promises of God are available to you, but you have to claim each one. And since you and I have an enemy who does not want us to claim God's promises for us, we are just going to have to fight for them. Jesus died so that we can obtain the promise. We do spiritual warfare to maintain the promise. Christ did His part; now you do yours. Release the spiritual warrior within!

The LORD shall fight for you, and ye shall hold your peace (Exodus 14:14, KJV).

ABOUT THE AUTHOR

Dr. Robert L. Bryan, Jr., is a prophet, pastor, teacher, and preacher who was called and commissioned by God at 18 years of age to minister the gospel of Jesus Christ throughout this nation and the world. He ministers with a strong prophetic voice and deliverance anointing.

In 1993 he organized the Sword of the Spirit Ministries, a New Testament, non-denominational church located in Forestville, Maryland. Since then, the ministry has grown to more than 31 outreaches. Dr. Bryan also founded the Spirit Life Institute, the educational branch of the ministry, which prepares and trains laypeople to do the work of the ministry. His radio ministry reaches across the Baltimore/Washington DC metropolitan area. He also has aired on the Black Entertainment Television (BET) network nationwide.

Dr. Bryan holds a Bachelor of Christian Education from Andersonville Baptist Seminary and a Master of Divinity and a Doctorate of Philosophy in Christian Education from Faith Bible College and Seminary.